Antique Flowers

Antique Flowers

A GUIDE TO USING

OLD-FASHIONED SPECIES IN

CONTEMPORARY GARDENS

BY KATHERINE WHITESIDE

PHOTOGRAPHY BY MICK HALES

WITH FOREWORDS BY JOHN FITZPATRICK

AND PENELOPE HOBHOUSE

DESIGN BY GAEL TOWEY

VILLARD BOOKS NEW YORK 1989

Title page: A profusion of antique flowers in a Somerset, England, garden.

Contents page: A blooming display in Somerset, England.

A RUNNING HEADS BOOK

Library of Congress Cataloging-in-Publication Data

Whiteside, Katherine, 1952–
  Antique flowers.

  Bibliography: p. 150
  Includes index.
  1. Flowers. 2. Plants, Ornamental. 3. Flowers—History. 4. Plants, Ornamental—History. 5. Flower gardening. I. Hales, Mick. II. Title.
SB407.W55   1989   635.9   88-40217
ISBN 0-394-57339-0

A N T I Q U E   F L O W E R S
was conceived and produced by
Running Heads Incorporated,
42 East 23rd Street,
New York, NY 10010

Editor: Sarah Kirshner
Designer: Gael Towey

Typeset by David E. Seham Associates
Color separation by Hong Kong Scanner Craft Company
Printed and bound in Singapore by Times Publishing Group

9 8 7 6 5 4 3 2

This book is dedicated to

Micah Devon Hales

and

August Somerset Hales.

We would like to thank the following people for their advice, encouragement, support, and assistance:

Alison Acker

David Beaumont

Joanna Bradshaw

Anne and Frank Cabot

Rudy Favretti

John Fitzpatrick

Keith and Mary Hales

Con and Dulce Hales

Marta Hallett

Peter Hatch

Michelle Hauser

Jill Herbers

Penelope Hobhouse

Bernard Jackson

Sarah Kirshner

Betty and Victor Luber

Michelle Mendola

Elizabeth McLean

Ellen Milionis

Senga Mortimer

John Nalley

Andrew Norton

Denise Otis

Marco Polo Stufano

Gael Towey

Carmen Vega

Harry and Becky Whiteside

We are also grateful to the following people and organizations who enthusiastically supported this project by allowing us to photograph their gardens:

Bartram Botanic Garden
Philadelphia, Pennsylvania

Chelsea Physic Garden
London, England

Robert Dash
Sagaponack, New York

Margery Fish Garden
Somerset, England

Fleurette Guilloz
Southampton, New York

Ryan Gainey
Decatur, Georgia

Keith and Mary Hales
Exeter, England

Memorial University
Botanical Garden
Newfoundland, Canada

Monticello
Charlottesville, Virginia

Emma Morgan
Long Island, New York

Elizabeth Murphy
Leeds, England

The Most Honourable Marchioness
of Salisbury
Hatfield, England

Michael and Lady Anne Tree
Shaftsbury, England

Rosemary Verey
Gloucestershire, England

Jane Watkins
Somerset, England

Wave Hill
Bronx, New York

Sarah Wolfe
Somerset, England

Contents

As surely as fabrics, hemlines, and hairstyles go in and out of fashion, garden flowers are also subject to fads and fancies. Trends in garden design, selection, and breeding for "improved" flower varieties, and larger-scale social changes such as industrialization have resulted in the neglect and sometimes complete disappearance of once-popular plants. Some antique garden flowers such as Goatsbeard, English Primrose, and Dame's Rocket have endured and appear today in the same form in gardens as they do in the fields and woods where they occur naturally. Other popular forms and colors such as double Wallflowers, white-flowered Honesty, and Shirley Poppies rarely occur in nature, but have been propagated and passed on to us by generations of dedicated gardeners. Many historic flowers are in our gardens right now, pleasing the senses—eye, nose, and palate—as they have done for centuries. In fact, these antique flowers often have superior fragrance and more interesting form and coloring than do their modern cousins. To cultivate them is a joy, but recognizing these plants for the valuable antiques they are opens a new dimension for appreciation—pleasure for the intellect.

As an enlightening and beautiful sourcebook of information, *Antique Flowers* provides an excellent starting place for both the experienced gardener and the novice to learn about the flowers appropriate for period gardens and to appreciate the versa-

FOREWORD

The View from the New World

Cleome hasslerana *growing at Thomas Jefferson's Monticello, in Charlottesville, Virginia.*

tility of these hardy favorites in any setting.

As director of the Thomas Jefferson Center for Historic Plants, I have a particular enthusiasm for this book. The Center was opened to the public in 1987 as an outgrowth of the extensive garden restoration at Monticello, Thomas Jefferson's home. Its objectives are the collection, documentation, propagation and distribution of plants grown in American gardens from colonial times up to the early twentieth century. *Antique Flowers* makes a valuable contribution to this heretofore neglected

field by bringing it to the attention of a wider audience. Katherine Whiteside's fresh, thought-provoking commentary, and Mick Hales's rich photographs reveal the special qualities of each historic flower in ways that any number of "seed catalogue" presentations fail to do.

The style of nomenclature used in *Antique Flowers* is as follows: botanical names conform to the standard reference, *Hortus Third,* and common names follow. For the sake of clarity, common names for specific plants are capitalized (Chimney Bellflower, Iceland Poppy, Maiden Pink), while common names for groups of plants are not (bellflowers, poppies, pinks).

Antique flowers are certainly not obscure botanical rarities; everyone from the beginner to the expert will recognize some of the plants in this book. All of them have been grown in American gardens and they represent tangible connections to our gardening past. I am confident that *Antique Flowers* will provide gardeners and flower lovers with another way of seeing and enjoying familiar plants—from the historical perspective—and open a door to some new acquaintances as well. Surely you will never look at a flower in quite the same way once you've learned something of its odyssey through the ages.

JOHN T. FITZPATRICK
Monticello
Charlottesville, Virginia

The title *Antique Flowers* is reminiscent of the ideals of English Pre-Raphaelites and the Arts and Crafts Movement of the late nineteenth century. A hundred years in cultivation has been chosen as a criterion for a plant's inclusion in this book; this sets a date in the 1880s, a time when English painters and poets, and a new generation of "old-fashioned" gardeners were beginning to stress the charm of well-loved cottage-garden flowers. They were portrayed in sentimental paintings and illuminated children's stories in which hollyhocks, honeysuckle, lilies, and old roses scrambled and tumbled over medieval arbors and cottage porches. In the nineteenth century, when extravagant bedding-out was fashionable in both England and North America, these older plants had been relegated to the kitchen garden or survived only in the gardens of more modest homes.

Fortunately, a new breed of gardeners and garden writers were active in re-establishing the charm and desirability of the older flowers. The writers William Robinson and Gertrude Jekyll suggested ways to use the old flowers in both the formal garden and in more natural settings. As a result, the Edwardian garden in England reached heights of floral beauty that have seldom been surpassed.

Katherine Whiteside works with many of the same hardy flowers that influential gardeners were using at the turn of the century. She has

FOREWORD

The View from the Old World

A view of Penelope Hobhouse's gardens at Tintinhull House in Somerset, England.

made a personal choice of old favorites; this is no criticism, in fact it is a bonus. Too many books seek to be comprehensive and in doing so become bland; I welcome being told a lot about selected subjects. As an English reader, I find Katherine Whiteside's book refreshing; *Antique Flowers* contains nuances of taste and fashion which, as a gardener, I look forward to exploring and certainly pondering over. I have to remind myself that some of our most prized garden plants from the New World are thought of as undesirable weeds by American gardeners. English gar-

deners love and need all these plants; American gardeners in turn treasure exotic flora which, in their common species and forms, seem of less value in European gardens. Fortunately, all are included in *Antique Flowers.*

I can confidently recommend this book to both English and American gardeners; indeed, I can extend this to gardeners all over the world. We live in an age when the relatives of our garden flowers, those still living in the wild, are threatened hourly by man's greed in destroying natural habitats. In America, some of the earliest introductions from the New World to European gardens are now so scarce in the wild that original plant species have to be reintroduced.

Antique Flowers is a cheerful evocation of the need for conservation; it is also timely because it serves as an *aide-mémoire* to plants that may be threatened; it sets them in a historical context as well as describing their medicinal and culinary uses. For those in charge of garden restorations it is informative, but more than that, *Antique Flowers* brings plants and their enjoyment alive. Plants are living and growing, and no garden should become a museum for period planting. Katherine Whiteside conveys a plant's charms; by doing so she encourages us to know and then grow the best of the old garden flowers.

PENELOPE HOBHOUSE
Tintinhull House
Somerset, England

L ike the majority of gardeners today, my favorite flowers could be loosely characterized as "old-fashioned." But modern gardeners, who have become increasingly sophisticated during this decade's gardening renaissance, have every right to question the meaning of the term. Does it describe flowers of the last century, the last decade, or the last year? For our purposes, *Antique Flowers* includes only those flowers which have been in gardens for at least one hundred years. Many of the flowers here are those that charmed the dreary lives of medieval peasants, or were the food and medicine of Colonial Americans, or were inspiration to poets, painters, kings, and presidents throughout the ages.

The term "old-fashioned" also brings up an important consideration we had in creating this book. Like every other commodity man touches, flowers are subject to the whims of fashion. In the past, when various old flowers went out of favor like last year's debutantes, many simply packed up their faded foliage and rumpled petals and disappeared forever. Many gardeners have experienced the frustration of trying to obtain flowers they remember seeing in their grandmother's gardens; it is a shame that some of these old favorites are now unavailable.

But all the antique flowers in this book are alive and growing in gardens today. You may find many you

Plant exploration continues. Seeds for dark blue Columbine, ABOVE, *were collected within the last decade by Royal Horticultural Society members trekking in Nepal.*

haven't seen in decades, and rediscover others you had no idea were so venerable. Right from the start, we decided it was a bit unfair to print luscious photographs and sing the praises of flowers that were impossible for the amateur gardener to obtain or cultivate. Since the purpose of *Antique Flowers* is to encourage, not to frustrate, you will find that there is a list of sources in the appendix for the plants we include. Also, we have been careful to choose plants that exhibit the sturdy, no-nonsense beauty which enlivened gardens of the past.

Everybody has a personal vision

of Paradise, and recently one of my friends expounded upon his idea of Heaven. "It will be wonderful because I will get to have the garden I have always wanted, with all my favorite flowers blooming all at once. I won't have to wait for spring, summer, or autumn, because daffodils, roses, and sunflowers will be there all the time." Although it sounded appealing to me at first, I soon realized that this Heaven would not be quite complete. Besides all my favorite flowers, my Paradise would also include my favorite garden people, so that I could have the company of those who have grown, studied, and loved flowers since the beginning of time. Obviously this idea, while pleasantly whimsical when I consider those who have already departed, is probably not so appealing to my friends who are alive and busy with twenty-year garden plans.

Since the days of the ancient Persians, gardeners have openly admitted to trying to create a bit of Paradise while still on Earth, so I hope it doesn't sound big-headed to say that creating *Antique Flowers* was a bit like my idea of Elysium. In this book there are many favorite flowers which, thanks to the magic of Mick Hales's photography, are all blooming at the same time. In Mick's photographs, however, each flower is not uniformly, impossibly perfect. Instead, he allows the plant's true character to show, and in so doing, expresses his respect for nature and his love for flowers.

And, because other flower lovers are an integral part of my heavenly ideal, you will find that *Antique Flowers* contains the ruminations, frustrations, and illuminations of centuries of favorite garden writers. Not only will you read the words of Elizabethan writers such as Gerard and Parkinson, but you will also see photographs of the gardens and flowers they loved. You will read the words of Thomas Jefferson, third President of the United States and passionate gardener, and see the flowers and gardens at Monticello that inspired his happiest moments. Twentieth-century English gardeners such as William Robinson and Margery Fish will share flower opinions with their American contemporaries like Alice Morse Earle and Elizabeth Lawrence. Their practical, romantic, funny—and sometimes snobby—opinions about the flowers in this book are bound to get your green thumb twitching in anticipation.

There is a quote from William Cole's seventeenth-century book, *The Art of Simpling,* that explains the gardener's quest for knowledge about the plants he or she grows: "What a pleasure it is for a man (whom the ignorant think to be alone) to have plants speaking Greek and Latin to him and putting him in mind of stories which otherwise he would never think of."

Read, grow, and enjoy.

A comfortable garden chair and towering hollyhocks make a heavenly setting in an old-fashioned garden.

The Story

The history of gardens and plant introductions is a vast, fascinating subject capable of yielding a lifetime of pleasurable reading. This brief historical overview focuses upon the rich horticultural heritage shared by England and America, and concentrates on the demands and fashions that influenced how gardens looked and what flowers they contained. It's important to remember that every antique flower was once a brand-new introduction into the garden, whether it was transplanted from a nearby pasture or was carried from a Tibetan mountaintop. This is a look at how garden novelties became established favorites.

# of Antique Flowers

Humble Beginnings

T he Black Death may seem an odd topic to brood upon when wandering through the sweetness and light of a colorful cottage garden, but the very first English cottage gardens arose out of the devastation wrought upon Europe by the fourteenth-century plague. The Black Death killed one-third of Europe's population, and with workers in demand and abandoned land plentiful, the slavery of the serfs slowly came to an end.

Freed slaves became tenant farmers, a pattern repeated throughout history, and although they still faced back-breaking poverty, these peasants slowly began to form an identity separate from their former masters. It seems that whenever human beings have respite from wars, slavery, or devastating illnesses, they settle down at home and invent labor-saving devices. The first tiny, rudimentary cottage gardens made by the English country people were nothing more than timesavers. Every flower of the field, each untamed plant of the riverbank, had a special meaning or use to the people of the medieval age, and considerable effort must have been expended every day to collect plants to season the soup or to spice up a romance. At some point, someone realized it would be a great convenience to grow a few plants near the doorway, which is how that now old favorite, the cottage garden, came into being.

E very plant in the early cottage garden had a purpose, but once flowers were so close at hand, it was impossible for even the most "rude mechanical" to ignore their beauty. As Roy Genders points out in his comprehensive book *The Cottage Garden and the Old-Fashioned Flowers:* "The plants of the first cottage gardens were almost the only possessions of the countryman, and he cared for them as those of a latter age care for possessions of the home." The day of the ornamental cottage garden was centuries away, but already the *need* for plants was finding delightful companionship with the *desire* for flowers.

Armeria maritima, *Sea Pink, shown growing in Cornwall, England, was an early healing herb that became a popular edging plant in the 1600s.*

Growing Sophistication

Nowadays, whirlpools and designer kettles express status for some, while yachts and helicopters are required by others. The grand are affected by trends and fashion as much as everyone else, so the English nobles who built great gardens during the seventeenth century put tremendous effort into commissioning splendid designs and obtaining fabulous flowers. No expense was spared in creating fashionable knot gardens, which were beautifully shaped by low hedges cleverly planted to look like green ribbons. Within the spaces created by the hedges were the rarest and choicest flowers available.

Plant explorers were dispatched to Holland and France, the trendy garden spots in those days, to obtain and carry back to England the non-native, or exotic, flowers that had become quite the rage. Sending plant hunters to Europe was certainly exciting, but nothing could top the expense and danger of sending someone all the way across the Atlantic to the newly discovered Americas to collect a treasure of new flowers. As the latest flower arrived on the scene from abroad, it was plonked into a bed with no regard for the restrictions (height, blooming time, and color coordination) that became hard and fast garden law much later.

As is often the case, the wherewithal of the wealthy eventually benefited the rest of society. The new plants that had been acquired for grand gardens trickled down and finally landed in more modest gardens, too. Her ladyship might direct the gardener to remove and discard some "old-fashioned things" from a bed to make way for something new from a distant place. But that gardener, and probably his father before him, had cossetted and enjoyed those old things for years, so rather than throw the plants on the compost heap, he would "save" them for his own garden. Thus, the gardens of

the humble welcomed the cast-offs of the grand and became depositories of old-fashioned favorites.

In the splendid gardens of the rich, flowers were often treasured more for the curiosity they aroused than the beauty they evoked. Seventeenth-century nobles spent considerable time visiting one another's estates, and the most lavish display of rare Dutch bulbs in Lord Flora's country garden was certain to be as exciting a topic for gossips as the mistress he kept in town.

The year 1629 was a banner one for John Parkinson. Not only did he attain the enviable position of Royal Botanist to Charles I, but he also published his

The gardens at Hatfield House in Hertfordshire, England, were created early in the seventeenth century.

best-seller, *Paradisi in Sole Paradisus Terrestris.* Although the title seems a little high-brow today, the modern reader should know that it is actually a delightful pun on the author's name, as it translates into English as "Park in Sun: An Earthly Paradise." The importance of this volume is enormous because, in essence, it was the first pretty, popular garden book to explore plants as objects of beauty rather than as sources of cures for wens, dropsy, or other complaints. It was a book about the pleasure garden, aimed at a well-to-do audience. Centuries after its publication,

it remains an invaluable reference for all garden enthusiasts.

Parkinson lived until 1650, long enough to greet the tide of New World plants that soon became the rage in English gardens. Although he was able to obtain many of the new imports, his own garden, containing the best of several generations' favorite flowers—pinks, tulips, and campanulas—would have already been considered old-fashioned by the very trendy. As one old gentleman of the period complained: "One need only to declare a flower to have come from America to make it immediately sought after." American flowers were difficult to obtain, and expensive. What more could one ask for when creating a fad?

At Hatfield, precisely formed beds
contain a delightful jumble of flower
treasures, including hundreds of
dianthus varieties. The pleached lime
walk was a later addition to the
Jacobean garden.

Starting Over in America

Flower fads had very little impact upon the plants that colonists of the 1600s took with them to the New World. Fashion meant nothing to the earnest young Englishwoman headed for an uncivilized land where, armed only with herbs, she would have to cope with illness, accident, birth, and death. The dooryard gardens of the colonies were filled with plants for food and for medicine, and as life gradually became more settled, the settlers explored their fields for new plants to add to the larder and medicine chest. Gradually the garden palette of plants increased, and within a few years, prospering colonists wrote home to brag about the wealth of plants in their new land.

As the European kings and companies who financed western exploration gradually realized that there was, sadly, no gold lying around the beaches of North America, some other material of exchange had to be considered. America's lush vegetation gradually became its treasury, and among the early settlers it was the Quakers who promoted the exchange of this commodity in the most organized fashion.

Quakers were respected for their scientific thirst, admired for their love for the natural world, famed for their abhorrence of politics, trusted for their scrupulous honesty, and probably envied for what we would now call their "networking system."

The efficiency of the Quakers in spreading the good news about American plants rivaled any modern

public relations effort. Early collections of American plant material caused so much excitement in Europe that it soon became a matter of course, when a ship left a European port for any destination at all, that there was someone on board anxious to do some plant exploring.

The Whipple House garden, LEFT, *in Ipswich, Massachusetts. Quaker John Bartram's garden,* ABOVE, *in Philadelphia is the oldest surviving botanic garden in America.*

Plants for Science

~

Juxtaposing fashion trends and the search for knowledge is rare, but flower fancies have also affected the way doctors and scientists look at plants.

Until the middle of the sixteenth century, physicians used ancient texts such as Dioscorides' *De Materia Medica,* written about A.D. 60, to guide them through the mysteries of botanical cures. These texts were almost always a haphazard mixture of popular myth and personal opinion, and had very little to do with experimentation or actual observation. Healing theories abounded, and one, known as the Doctrine of Signatures, marked the nadir of medical history. This theory, popularized in sixteenth-century Italy, proposed that all plants were put on Earth for the good of Man, and that each plant provided clues as to the way it was meant to be used. A red flower might have meant that the plant was good for the blood, a blue flower was perhaps good for blue eyes, and a speckled leaf was expected to cure spots of all sorts. Simply put, there was little separation between magic

~

Chelsea Physic Garden, located in the heart of London, was one of the first Old World botanic gardens and remains a vital center for plant research today.

and medicine, and it seems miraculous that unhealthy people sometimes had the luck to survive their "cures."

At the beginning of the seventeenth century, about the same time that those grand English gardens were becoming the rage, herbal healing began to take on a slightly more do-it-yourself edge. The old monastery gardens, where monks had studied and grown healing herbs, had been destroyed a generation before during the reign of Henry VIII, forcing common people to become more self-reliant about growing medicinal plants. Plant books written in English, rather than Latin, became available. One of the first great herbals written in English, John Gerard's *Herball or Generall Historie of Plants,* was published in 1597 and remains today an important record of plant use in that century.

Although Gerard cribbed a lot of his text and illustrations from several sources, he did, in fact, know a considerable amount about plants. He was a hard-working gardener, and his garden in London contained over one thousand plants, which he recorded in his *Catalogus* of 1596.

(This *Catalogus* is a bit of bragging to which any gardener can relate, but it was also the first time someone had bothered to record every plant, mundane or rare, in any one garden. This is why an inordinate number of plants have 1596 as their date of introduction; any earlier date is often impossible to document.)

Another herbal written at this time became very popular in Colonial America. Nicholas Culpeper's *The English Physician or Herball* was published in 1652. The modern reader cannot help but notice that the right phases of the moon still seemed to be critical to curing a patient in Culpeper's time. Times were changing, however, and in 1673 The Society of Apothecaries of London banded together to plant the first small plots of

~

The beds are organized by genus at Chelsea and the collections are extensive. Philip Miller (1691–1771) was Chelsea's dynamic head gardener for years and sent wildflower seeds to Bartram in Philadelphia and cotton seeds to Georgia.

herbs for Chelsea Physic Garden on the banks of the Thames. Although not the first physic garden, it was a place where plants would be studied systematically and scientifically and the art of healing slowly moved out of the realm of magic.

By 1753, Carl Linnaeus was pushing his *Species Plantarum* as the easiest and most efficient way to name plants as they poured into Europe from unfamiliar regions of the world. Lest we forget that science is a lively art, Linnaeus developed his system of classifying plants by counting the female and male parts of their flowers. This so titillated a growing fan club of amateur botanists that botany became a sort of parlor game, and prose and poetry were written to commemorate the new craze.

The Golden Age of Botany was in full swing by the end of the eighteenth century, and in a single twenty-five-year period (1789–1814) the English royal family welcomed 7,000 new plants into its private botanic garden at Kew. The quest for new plants, whether in the name of science or in the search for status, was showing no signs of diminishing.

The American Garden Grows Up

Although Botany's Golden Age reached its peak in the late 1700s, a time when English-American relations were more than slightly strained, this did not stop the author of the Declaration of Independence from making an English garden tour. In 1786, Thomas

Jefferson, a dedicated gardener, visited several gardens in the counties surrounding London, and, as many other Americans after him have done, returned from abroad to his own garden determined to make changes. Jefferson's mountaintop garden at Monticello near Char-

The nineteenth century saw the blooming of ornamental gardening in America. Thomas Jefferson used his garden at Monticello as a horticultural proving ground for establishing an American garden vernacular.

lottesville, Virginia, and the horticultural experimentation that its harsher climate inspired led the way toward developing a garden style that gradually became more American than English. Jefferson promoted the use of American flowers, and, as the third president of the young na-

tion, he used his power to encourage plant exploration in the uncharted wilderness of the American West. When the Lewis and Clark expedition returned in 1806, many new American plants were introduced to Monticello, then Philadelphia, and eventually made their way to London.

Fashion's Full Circle

By the early nineteenth century American plant material had been a rage for quite some time, and fashions being what they are, it was inevitable that Something New just had to show up soon. Plants from the Far East were quite exciting for a while, but finally nothing struck the fancy of the truly sophisticated Victorian gardener like the fad for delicate plants from warm climates such as California, Brazil, and Mexico. These tender plants required glasshouses, trained gardeners, and reserve stocks—they were expensive garden toys. Nothing else would do but to impress others with the huge quantities of these plants that one could produce. Graceful exotics were bred to produce uniform, compact shapes, and these squat cushions were then transplanted, by the hundreds, into large beds laid out like flat carpets or ribbons. Every little plant was expected to bloom with sickening fervor; once it paused, it would be yanked up by the roots and replaced with another.

But, while some must acquire every new video game on the market, others find that wooden rocking horses and rag dolls, sturdy and infinitely more charming, are more apt to capture long-term delight. During the middle of the last century there arose the garden equivalent of the rocking horse and rag doll contingent, a colorful and outspoken group that came to the rescue of old-fashioned flowers. This admittedly privileged and well-published assemblage had the great good sense to tap into a wonderful but virtually voiceless network of plant-savers: the poor, who had never been able to afford faddish flowers; the clergy, who often had enormous vicarage gardens and who disdained the whims of fashion; and the Quakers, who had simply carried on, century after century, as great gardeners, botanists, and plant collectors. William Robinson published *The English Flower Garden* with great success in 1883, about the same time that the Parkinson Society was founded "to search out and cultivate old flowers which have become scarce."

William Robinson's work influenced garden style on both shores of the Atlantic. American and English

Margery Fish, once called the Champion of Weeds, saved many old cottage favorites. Her restored garden in Somerset, England, is open to the public, and the beauty of plants on these and the following pages testify to her lifetime of dedication to the old-fashioned flower.

garden writers encouraged others to use sturdy, lovely flowers from the past. Nearer to our own times, English writers such as Gertrude Jekyll and Vita Sackville-West, and Americans Alice Morse Earle and Elizabeth Lawrence, whose names all sound appropriately old-fashioned, caused quite a stir in their day with their romantic, scented gardens. They urged gardeners to return to an appreciation for the individual characters of flowers and, in very basic terms, this is why our grandmothers had such lovely gardens.

Today, many new organizations are being formed to save, grow, and promote flowers that fashion may have ignored for centuries. Let us hope that this movement, enriched by centuries of garden history, will accomplish its goals. Sustained by our generation, this would be a worthy contribution to all gardens.

The gardeners and writers on the pages of this book, champions of old-fashioned gardening and devout students of plant and flower cultivation, are the heroes and heroines of antique gardening today. It is through their work with plants and their written records that we have been handed a bountiful legacy of lovely flowers for our own gardens.

An old-fashioned garden by the sea on Long Island, New York. A gardener can create a glorious array by making artistic and intelligent choices when combining antique and modern plant material.

Successful gardening is not dogmatic. Here,
an English garden plan combines Tudor as
well as Moghul influences and the whole scheme
is united with lush, old-fashioned
plants and flowers.

*Exuberant plantings, as opposed to
highly manicured beds, allow flowers
to show their wild beauty. Even tiny
gardens grow more lovely when
allowed to run riot.*

This gardener collects unusual seeds and plants from old or abandoned gardens in the rural South and propagates them in his garden in the suburbs of Decatur, Georgia. He also finds farmers' market bulletins good sources for locating old-time plants.

The rear of the house, ABOVE. and flowers spilling into the street in the front, OPPOSITE. Next to the house, a former nursery provides room for greenhouses, large plantings and a kitchen garden, RIGHT and BELOW.

Raising beautiful flowers to use in splendid bouquets can become
a cottage industry for an enterprising gardener. This garden near
Southampton, New York, contains many antique varieties.

Modern gardeners may choose from a vast palette of lovely flowers, yet increasing numbers search for the sturdy hardiness, delicate beauty, and sweet scent of antique varieties. The following Plant Portraits introduce (or recall) garden favorites that have been grown and loved for at least a century. Words of encouragement from the past join photographs of today's gardens to show even the most inexperienced how to grow and enjoy these delightful and desirable flowers: our living antiques.

A Portfolio of

Antique Species

Lady's Mantle, native to Europe, Asia, and Greenland, has been a garden favorite for centuries. Its fancy appearance, with flowers like constellations of tiny yellow stars above vandyked leaves, belies the constitution of a workhorse.

Lady's Mantle can work wonders for the disposition of anyone who gets grumpy on rainy days. That industrious gardener, plantsman, and author E. A. Bowles (1865–1954) would grudgingly stop his horticultural chores only for the worst of

name. Modern gardeners, however, are increasingly turning to Alchemilla for more cheery reasons. This hardy perennial does well in poor, dry soil, doesn't mind a bit of shade, and will seed itself attractively into rock crevices. Its lovely leaves unfold like green fans between paving stones, and it makes a wonderful carpet under roses.

The form of Alchemilla most widely available today is the large-leaved *Alchemilla vulgaris* which was introduced in 1874. Graham Stuart

Alchemilla vulgaris Rosaceae

LADY'S MANTLE

downpours. Then, as he described in *My Garden in Summer,* he would move to a garden shelter and sit upon an old church pew with "a knobby pattern carved on the back that [was] not comfy to lean against." One can almost see the old dear fidgeting away ("it is not pleasant to sit for long"), but he wrote that Lady's Mantle offered him solace during these regrettably unproductive moments. "It is the leaves which are the notable features. . . . [They are] of a very tender shade of greyish-green and covered with fine, silky hairs which help their cup-like shape to hold raindrops glittering like drops of quicksilver."

Long before Mr. Bowles's time, medieval alchemists noted the silvery water on the leaves of Lady's Mantle

A graceful flower arrangement includes Lady's Mantle and a jumble of other antique flowers, LEFT. *Lady's Mantle grows amid paving stones in an English garden,* ABOVE.

and collected this liquid to add to their gold-making recipes. The Arabic word describing this group of dreamers, *Alkemelyeh,* was later Latinized to make the generic name, *Alchemilla.*

In Elizabethan times there was a great demand for the plant, as it was used as a cure for just about every woman's ailment you could possibly

Thomas, distinguished author, artist, and Gardens Consultant to the English National Trust, wrote in *Perennial Garden Plants* that Lady's Mantle will "grow anywhere, except in a bog," but one place it probably should not be grown is in the rock garden. One spindly, store-bought seedling can grow to a breadth of up to three feet (1 m) across, soon turning an alpine showplace into an exclusive Lady's Mantle show.

Although the stems of Alchemilla look a bit prickly, the whole plant is actually downy-soft and a pleasure to use in flower arrangements. If anything could be more beautiful than a single pink rosebud in a vase, it is that same flower and vase, decorated with one magic leaf of Lady's Mantle.

The flowers of this plant offer you the opportunity surreptitiously to probe the hidden political leanings of your friends. When asked what the flower resembles, some say that its petals are like the extended wings of eagles, with the curved spurs resembling a fierce neck and head. More peaceful types see the same shape as a gathering of doves drinking from a bowl. Aquilegia comes from the Latin *aquila* (eagle), and columbine from *columba* (dove). But if you prefer to avoid sneaky psychological-political assessments, just call the plant Granny's Bonnet and discuss instead the bygone elegance of women's fashions.

Some species of *Aquilegia* are native to Europe and some to North America. *Aquilegia canadensis,* from the eastern United States, was sent to Hampton Court in 1640 by John Tradescant the Younger, but, frankly speaking, it's a bit tricky to use in the garden due to its bold red-and-yellow flowers. One either likes this color combination or one doesn't; but if you are striving to create an American wildflower garden, the colors of *A. canadensis* may be toned down a bit by planting it beside white flowers.

If North American natives aren't a major concern in the garden plan, stick with the wild European Columbine, *Aquilegia vulgaris*. It comes in pink, blue, mauve, white, or dark

COLUMBINE
GRANNY'S BONNET

Aquilegia vulgaris

purple and has pretty gray-green leaves. The flower comes in single and double forms, but that venerable arbiter of taste English poet and artist William Morris (1834-1896) warned against the double forms because, "the clustering of doves [!] is unmistakable and distinct in the single, but in the double runs into mere tatters."

Just about every garden in England has stands of Columbine. They were once used in that country to "remove obstructions from the liver." However, *Aquilegia* belongs to the poisonous Buttercup Family, and Linnaeus wrote that overzealous dosing of the remedy often proved fatal, so one must assume that as unfortunate liver patients died out, so did this dangerous custom.

A. vulgaris is uncommon in American gardens, a sad oversight because these flowers are very easy to grow and make a lovely show. Alice Morse Earle wrote in *Old Time Gardens* (1901) that she could remember back to 1870 when a pale blue columbine bloomed in her mother's New England garden, "where it grew and thrived and was vastly admired," and it seems high time to start a revival of this plant on the western shore of the Atlantic.

A. vulgaris is happy anywhere, sun or shade, as long as it doesn't get too dry. The plant comes into leaf very early, which is useful to

Columbines are very popular in England and can be easily grown in America. Following the tradition of centuries, pink and blue varieties thrive in a garden near Leeds, England, OPPOSITE *and* ABOVE.

cover bare earth in the spring. Its foliage is pretty, with softly scalloped leaves sometimes tinged with purple. Aquilegia looks lovely when planted with ferns, or one can start a succession of blue flowers by companion planting blue Columbine with Canterbury Bells. The white form of the flower can be used with irises, such as Orris (*Iris* × *germanica* var. *florentina*), Candytuft (*Iberis sempervirens*),

and white Rugosa Roses for a softly colored border.

Columbines are prolific and within several years of your first planting you may have many extra plants to use as fillers or to give to friends. The seedheads are pretty enough to use in dried flower arrangements, but if you want to use them for spreading European Columbine to other areas of your garden, as soon as they ripen, shake the small black seeds wherever more plants are wanted. If you're growing fancy hybrid forms of Columbine in the same garden, *A. vulgaris* will quickly crossfertilize and dominate the hybrids. One antique gardening encyclopedia recommends planting the separate kinds far apart and covering the flowers with fine muslin to prevent interbreeding, but this is of doubtful aesthetic value. Why not let them intermingle and see what happens?

Another potential problem with columbines may be the presence of leaf miner, a tiny larva that tunnels through the leaves and makes winding yellow trails. An excellent way to control this pest is to cut down the foliage after the seeds are mature. Pale, pretty new leaves will appear by autumn.

Don't let the fear of a little larva prevent you from using *Aquilegia*. They are very garden-worthy flowers, and George Nicholson of the Royal Gardens at Kew wrote in 1884, "Too much praise can scarcely be lavished upon this elegant genus of plants."

Ranunculaceae

GOATSBEARD

Goatsbeard is a North American and Eurasian native that traveled to English gardens as early as 1633. Experts have changed its botanical name several times, but seem to have settled, at least for the moment, upon *Aruncus dioicus*.

The Greek term *dioicus* (two houses) means that the male and female flowers of Goatsbeard bloom on separate plants. The male flower is more upright and showy, and the female flower, softer in form, produces seedheads useful for dried flower arrangements. Arthur Tysilio Johnson, a writer who gardened in Wales, bragged that "the husbands are . . . very much handsomer in their plumes than the more drooping tasselled ladies, and they are happy enough unconsciously waving their magnificent beards to an unresponding world."

This rather sexist description dismisses the softer charms of the lady Goatsbeard, but both genders are wonderful and it seems rather tough that Mr. Johnson pictures a world unresponsive to the beauty and vigor of this hardy perennial.

Aruncus grows in any soil and doesn't care if it has sun or shade. If in a moist place, such as the bank of a pond, this plant can reach six feet (2 m) in height. A drier situation

Aruncus dioicus Rosaceae

will not faze Aruncus, but it probably will stop growing somewhere around four feet (1–2m).

Goatsbeard may be used in the wild garden, in borders, or even as a bold planting on a lawn. This is one of those large plants that gives great return for very little effort.

Wherever you decide to plant Aruncus, be sure to mark its place. It is slow to wake in the spring, and it would be a shame to mistake its location as another little grave to be replanted. When the leaves do appear, they are broad and handsome and will quickly make a tall light green mound lasting for many months. Sometime in the summer, Aruncus will start producing great plumes, around eight inches long, decorated with hundreds of cream-colored flowers, and, a month or two later, will make up for its lazy spring start by producing attractive yellow autumn foliage.

If one is very lucky, Goatsbeard's hay-scented flowers will appear at the same time as those of their relatives, the shrub roses. These plants are very pretty together and their cut flowers make big, old-fashioned bouquets that would certainly cost a fortune from the florist.

Aruncus seems fairly free from disease, but do post a lookout for sawfly larvae. These pests will eat the leaves into skeletons but can be controlled by simply tearing up their meal ticket. Cut the foliage down to the ground and, within a short time, new, unchewed leaves will appear and Aruncus will arise again.

Aruncus is a dramatic addition to enormous arrangements, OPPOSITE. *In full glory in an American garden,* ABOVE, *and with attractive buds in an English one,* BELOW.

POT MARIGOLD
GOLDS
RUDDLES

There are many plants that claim the name of marigold as their own, and perhaps the most well known are the French and African Marigolds (*Tagetes patula* and *T. erecta*). But the cheerful old workhorse Calendula definitely predates these upstarts, and is the marigold that is referred to in historical texts.

John Gerard, that devoted six-teenth-century gardener, wrote that "the marigold is called calendula, it is seene in floure in the Calends al-most every moneth." The *calend* was the first day of a month in the an-cient Roman calendars; Gerard is re-ferring to the belief that this plant flowers on the first day of every month the year round, and it may bloom continuously in warmer areas of Great Britain. In America, Calen-dula flowers all year in warm areas such as in California, where it has escaped from gardens and grows wild. In colder regions the gardener must be content with a flowering season from July to frost.

Calendulas are useful in the larder, and there are many mouthwatering recipes using the flowers in every-thing from soup to nuts. Cooked petals may replace saffron in sauces

Calendula

and, uncooked, add color and spice to salads. During the seasonal glut, petals may be picked, dried slowly, and stored for later use.

Marigold cheese is an old English delicacy that uses dried petals and "the milk of seven cows and the cream from the milk of seven other cows." If one chicken is more readily available than fourteen cows, an English cookbook from 1588 recommends that a delicious white broth be made for poultry from Calendula, Marjoram, Parsley, and Thyme. Another treat that should be given a try is venison seasoned with Calendula and Mint, followed by marigold pudding (similar in idea to plum pudding), accompanied by a sauce of rosewater, sugar, and soft butter.

There are other more fanciful uses for the plant. One book from the sixteenth century contains a Calendula concoction to "enable one to see the fairies," and its usefulness in love potions is also asserted. The Scottish anthropologist Sir James Frazer (1854–1941) reported that it was a Balkan tradition for a peasant girl to dig up the soil on which her sweetheart's footsteps had fallen and pot marigolds in it as a symbol of enduring love. Charles I, the English king executed in 1649, complained that "The marigold observes the sun/ More than my subjects me have done," causing royalists to use the flower as an indication of loyalty.

Calendula ointment is very good for cuts, burns, bruises, and sores, and in 1897, Dr. W.T. Fernie wrote in *Herbal Simples* that the flowers were used on a large scale by American surgeons to treat wounds and injuries during the Civil War. There is even an unsubstantiated report that during World War I, Gertrude Jekyll (1843–1932), one of the twentieth century's most influential gardeners, devoted a large part of her famous Sussex garden to raising Calendulas. She harvested bushels of the flowers and sent them to first-aid stations in France to be used in dressings for wounded soldiers.

Having said so much about the practical uses of Calendulas, it is also important to stress their sturdy beauty in the garden. They are good in the border, the kitchen garden, and are suitable for containers. Calendula self-sows happily, so although an annual, it usually needs to be planted only once. The flowers range from pale yellow to deep orange in both single and double varieties. Garden books from the turn of the century note varieties such as 'Orange King' and 'Lemon Queen,' but some favorites from the 1930s had such up-to-date monikers as 'Meteor' and 'Radio.'

The Calendula is a foolproof plant that thrives with very little attention, even when faced with almost impossible conditions. Margery Fish saluted the Calendula and wrote that "there is something very satisfactory about these old friends with their rounded leaves, thick stems, and cheerful flowers. . . . Their scent is clean and astringent and it reminds one of a healthy, happy country woman."

With strong claim to being the true marigold, hardy Calendulas grow as well in Georgia, OPPOSITE, *as they do in chilly Newfoundland.* ABOVE, *they are photographed in Heirloom Garden at Memorial University Botanic Garden in St. Johns, Newfoundland.*

officinalis Compositae

that cathedrals rose above the fields and hovels of medieval towns like the magic mountains of fairy tales. Pilgrims could see their destination from quite far away, and, perhaps to savor the experience of the pilgrimage, they would often gather in small groups for rituals to mark the final miles. Relieved and exhilarated by the journey's promised end, those traveling to the Thomas à Becket shrine at Canterbury passed through fields of white flowers (most likely *C. trachelium*) ringing horse bells to announce their arrival, and, hopeful-

flowers in America was not until 1760, when a Boston newspaper advertised some of the plants for sale. However, it seems fairly safe to say that numerous colonial dooryard gardens of previous years "unofficially" enjoyed the rough, wavy-edged leaves and strong spikes of blue Canterbury Bells.

Several relatives of Canterbury Bells are worth mention. *Campanula rotundifolia* is the delicate Blue Harebell found wild in Scotland, and *Campanula pyramidalis* is the Chimney Bellflower, whose name is de-

CANTERBURY BELLS

Campanula medium

This genus is enormously popular, offering species with great diversity in size and form, with many suitable for garden use. One of the oldest and most beloved of the bellflowers is *Campanula medium,* long favored as a showy blue plant for the garden.

C. medium was known as Coventry Bells in the sixteenth and seventeenth centuries. Its current name, Canterbury Bells, first belonged to its cousin *Campanula trachelium,* a flower associated with an early religious custom at Canterbury Cathedral. No one is quite sure how the switch of plants and cathedrals was made, but the story of the original name is an interesting one.

To evoke the full romance of the flower's name, one must remember

Canterbury Bells, LEFT, *Foxgloves and Hollyhocks make up the flowering triumvirate of the midsummer garden. The single form and the Cup-and-Saucer form,* RIGHT, *also come in pink, white, rose, or purple.*

ly, their salvation. Just why *C. trachelium* gave up its romantic past to become known as Nettle-leaved Bellflower, and how Coventry Bells assumed the name Canterbury Bells are pieces of garden lore that have not found their way through the centuries.

"Canterburie bels" were included in the garden described by Estienne and Liébault in 1570, but the first documented use of these well-loved

Foxglove, is one of the last biennials to bloom in the season. Thorough watering, but not much else, is important. The flowers, although famous in blue, also come in pink, mauve, rose, and white.

A variety of *C. medium,* 'Calycanthema,' is the lovely old Cup-and-Saucer. One writer [Walter Brett, in *Your Garden's Flowers Illustrated* (1939)] strikes a Goldilocks-type complaint, saying that the single Canterbury Bells "are a little on the plain side," and the doubles "rather freakish in appearance," but that the

Alice Morse Earle, especially fond of blue flowers, wrote that Canterbury Bells "enrich the beauty and blueness of the garden." Richardson Wright, who was editor of *House & Garden* in the 1920s and author of several gardening books, once planned a lovely old-fashioned bor-

Campanulaceae

rived from its past popularity as a potted plant used to camouflage empty summertime hearths. *Campanula persicifolia* or Peach-bells is popular in the garden and *Campanula rapunculus,* once eaten as a salad, achieved notoriety as the rampion stolen from a witch's garden by a well-known fairy tale character. The poor thief only wanted the plant for his hungry pregnant wife, but the witch was furious and demanded that the baby be given to her at birth. The witch named the baby Rapunzel after *C. rapunculus* and later, of course, the child grew up to have famous golden hair.

Campanula medium is one of the finest biennials available and is quite hardy. It is an early grower and with

Other popular Campanulas include C. rapunculus, RIGHT, *from the fairy tale and* C. persicifolia, LEFT, *old-fashioned Peach-bells.*

～

Cup-and-Saucer form suited him just fine.

When raised from seed, Canterbury Bells do not flower in their first season. The seedlings should be transplanted to a shady spot and protected from rot over the winter. Moved to a sunny location in spring, the mature plants usually do not require staking and if more plants are not required, the deadheads can be removed promptly to prolong flowering.

der with a Rugosa Rose hedge as background, delphiniums in the next rows, lupines and Canterbury Bells massed in all shades, and Perennial Candytuft as an edging. His plan was that just as the lupines went over, the Canterbury Bells, delphiniums, and roses would appear. A less complicated plan was the colonial self-sowing garden of pinks, poppies, larkspur, and Canterbury Bells. But however the flower is used, remember that the romance and color of this plant are not easily replaced by any other.

The treasures of King Tutankha-men's tomb have entranced even the most jaded for generations. When this king died in his teens, his final resting place was piled with beautiful clothing, finely wrought jewelry, exquisite utensils and weapons—every imaginable object a young royal might require in the next life. Books and museums have cata-logued, photographed, and displayed the sumptuous golden plunder many times for a gawking public, but there was one small offering in the tomb that has escaped the attention of many viewers. Attached to Tut's second sarcophagus was a tiny wreath of olive leaves and—still intact after thousands of years—Cornflowers.

Cornflowers are part of a very large genus of 500 or so species. The botanical name (*Centaurea*) is a trib-ute to the mythical centaur Chiron, who used these flowers to heal a nasty wound. Chiron later taught the art of herbal healing to mankind, but his first experience seems to have been largely forgotten, because Cornflowers were ignored for centu-ries as medicinal plants. This may be because the flower was often con-

Clear blue Cornflowers are delightful to grow and ask for no attention at all. This gardener lets them self-seed throughout his garden and uses the dried flowers in delicate wreaths. This annual can stand heat and drought and will attract birds to the area.

fused in texts with Centaury, a pink member of the Gentian Family, so early herbalists perhaps thought that ignoring the plant altogether was the best way to avoid any mix-ups.

However, that notorious system of herbal medicine, the Doctrine of Signatures, eventually set upon a use

ged Sailor refers to the cottony foliage and slightly tattered appearance of the flowers, and Hurt-sickle to the tough stems that once ruined the cutting edges of the tools of unlucky harvesters.

Perhaps Cornflowers have many names for the same reason that some

Centaurea cyanus Compositae

for Cornflowers. With no scientific basis at all, practitioners of this method decided that since Cornflowers were blue, and as many English people in those days may have had blue eyes, Cornflowers were used as a cure for eye ailments. This cause was espoused to such a degree that by the eighteenth century, Cornflower water was considered not only a cure for eye problems, but also an optical strengthener. Variations of Break-Spectacle-Water were still on the market at the beginning of this century and thus the folk name Break-Your-Spectacles for Cornflowers was a promise worthy of a snake-oil salesman.

Blue Bottle is a folk name that refers to the similarity of shape between the flower and the wineskins of the Old Testament. Bachelor's-Button is also a common nickname, but since twenty-one other flowers share the same appellation, it is a bit too common for its own good. Rag-

CORNFLOWER

BACHELOR'S-BUTTON

BLUE BOTTLE

❧

Blue C. montana, A B O V E, *is a perennial antique Centaurea. Yellow* C. macrocephala, B E L O W, *is another perennial species.*

people seem to collect affectionate nicknames from their friends: Cornflowers have always been popular. They are often described as the bluest flower in the garden, and this southern European native is certainly easy to like as it flowers all summer without making a single demand. Seeds can be flung in the most offhand manner and soon silvery foliage will rise about two feet (61 cm) tall and produce ample supplies of lovely thistle-like flowers.

Cornflowers have been called lusty monopolists and ideally should be given plenty of space in the garden. A wild patch sown with Rye, Timothy, Field Poppies, and Cornflowers will produce year after year, and will attract goldfinches as well. Cornflowers make excellent arrangements and their color exactly matches old-fashioned blue Nankin china. Anyone who smirks about having weeds on the dining table should be reminded of the story of flowers fit for an Egyptian king.

Centranthus ruber Valerianaceae

RED VALERIAN

This is a wonderful plant to point out casually, using one of its more obscure common names. Many long-suffering guests, denied refreshment until after "a short walk around the garden before dark" have been instantly enlivened when the proud gardener identifies this hardy border plant by proudly announcing "Kiss-Me-Quick."

Luckily for guest and gardener, Centranthus flowers for a long time, usually from June to September. It has naturalized all over Europe on old walls, ruins, and rocky ground. One must be careful not to confuse Centranthus with another old favorite, *Valeriana officinalis,* called True Valerian. Centuries ago, *V. officinalis,* a powerful sedative, served the alarming dual purpose as a treatment for hysteria and as a very successful

In the restoration of Margery Fish's garden at East Lambrook Manor, Somerset, England, Red Valerian is mixed in beds with shrubs, climbers and other flowers, LEFT. *Though a Mediterranean native, Red Valerian has naturalized along the beaches of the Devonshire coast,* ABOVE.

rat bait. Unfortunate patients who received a dose of this Valerian probably stopped screaming for fear of what their breath might attract. Centranthus, the Valerian pictured here, was used in primitive embalming efforts, information that can only leave the modern gardener

thankful that he or she may grow either type of valerian and not have to worry about practical uses.

Centranthus is native to the Mediterranean. The name derives from the Greek words *kentron* (spur) and *anthos* (flower). It is hardy, and will happily thrive and multiply in very poor soil, especially where old plaster has been dumped or where chalk or lime makes life difficult for other types of plants. There are white, pink, mauve, and crimson varieties, and the stout woody stems reach two to three feet (60 cm to one meter) tall with no staking. The big flower panicles and attractive blue-green foliage are good for arrangements, but care must be taken not to bruise the stems—all aesthetic value will be seriously compromised by the resulting catty smell.

Cheiranthus cheiri Cruciferae

WALLFLOWER

Wallflowers are one of the oldest, sweetest, and most popular of garden flowers in England and on the Continent, yet American gardens seem oddly devoid of this wonderfully scented, early-blooming perennial. As a turn-of-the-century American gardening book notes: "Attractive as it is, gardens in this country have never had the success with the wall flower that it seems they ought to have."

The Wallflower's native habitat is the gentle climate of the Canary Islands and Madeira, so obviously this plant is a challenge for those gardeners who must cope with harsh winters. Wallflowers are so widely grown in England that it just doesn't seem like springtime until the air is filled with their scent. It seems high time for adventuresome American gardeners to take up the quest for Wallflower success.

The English Wallflower is one of the first harbingers of scented spring. Here the species type makes a bright splash of color at Monticello.

There is historical precedent for the challenge of North American Wallflower growing. In 1807, Thomas Jefferson wrote to Bernard McMahon, a Philadelphia seedsman and author of *The American Gardener's Calendar,* and asked him about growing Wallflowers at Monticello. McMahon was well respected as a reliable recorder of American gardening conditions. He sent Jefferson Wallflower seeds, but recommended that they be grown in pots and brought into the house for winter protection. Apparently this method was successful and Wallflowers are grown at Monticello to this day.

So why all the fascination with *Cheiranthus cheiri*? To any gardener interested in old flowers, the Wallflower has arguably one of the richest of documented histories. Lucius Junius Moderatus Columella, the Spanish-Roman author, wrote ten volumes that together comprise one of the very early Roman horticultural works. In addition to suggesting that all gardens should be surrounded by walls or hedges for privacy, with a statue of Priapus, the diety responsible for successful gardening, conspicuously displayed, Columella divides his list of plants into groups according to use. Wallflowers appear prominently on these ancient lists of ornamentals suitable for Roman enjoyment. Also, the ancient paradisiacal gardens of Persia—which featured the choicest trees, shrubs, and flowers—contained beds planted with Wallflowers.

By the end of the 1500s, Wallflowers were an important part of the skillful gardening then in vogue in France. In the sixteenth century Olivier de Serres wrote *Le Théâtre d'Agriculture,* which showed the garden divided into separate areas for food, fruit, herb, and flower growing. He recommended that flowers be grown in parterres—flat, elaborately shaped gardens outlined with low hedges, which were meant to be viewed from the upper stories of extravagant chateaux. Low-growing flowers such as Wallflowers, pinks, and violets were used in the spaces created by the parterre hedges.

There is no record of exactly when Wallflowers reached England, but by the sixteenth century they had so many common names in English that they must have been popular for quite a while. Some of these names, now commonly associated with other flowers, were: Gilliflower, Sweet William, Herte's Ease, Bloody Warrior, Yealowe Flower, and Viola Lutea. Francis Bacon wrote in his famous essay "Of Gardens" (1625) that Wallflowers should be planted under parlor windows where their scent could be enjoyed by those indoors. The English of Tudor times simply could not get enough of the flower. They used it in knot gardens that were similar to the French parterres, with short, shorn hedges laid out in elaborate shapes. Knots were "closed" if they were filled with flowers and "open" if they were filled with colored gravel. In another charming use of Wallflowers, the English made springtime bouquets of the blossoms. These hand-held posies probably comforted the olfactory sense in those smelly days and may also have been the source of the genus name: *kheir* means hand in Greek, and *anthos,* flower.

One of the most famous Wallflower stories is the romantic tale of the Maid of Neidpath, whose lack of knot-tying knowledge led to her untimely demise at the foot of a castle wall. Seventeenth-century English poet Robert Herrick wrote that she tried to make a rope to lower herself from a high window, "But the silken twist untied/ So she fell and

These larger-flowered wallflowers are typical of those that were bred in the early seventeenth century. They are among the first to bloom in this New York garden.

bruised and died." The highly unsuitable suitor who had tempted her to such parental defiance, Scott of Tushielaw, sadly picked a sprig from a Wallflower near where she died, stuck it in his hat, and became a roving minstrel of such great repute that his signature Wallflower was later to become a symbol of fidelity in adversity.

Some old books say that Wallflowers are easily grown in moist soil with moderate shade, but most agree that Cheiranthus is not really winter hardy. Potted plants may be wintered in cold frames or in the garage. In milder climates, of course, the plant can stay outdoors all year and may surprise you with winter bloom. Although strictly a perennial, treat this plant as a biennial in mild climates—planting one summer or fall and waiting for flowers to appear the second year—and as an annual in the north—purchasing second-year plants ready to bloom that season. Remove the tip of the tap root when planting out to encourage more side roots, and never allow the plant to dry out. The bloom goes on for quite a while, providing that deadheading is strictly practiced.

Thomas Jefferson once said that "the greatest service which can be rendered any country is to add a useful plant to its culture." Although he was speaking of more practical crops than his Wallflowers, it is nice to know that this most famous of early American horticultural experimenters deemed Cheiranthus worthy of his attention.

Chrysanthemum parthenium

Feverfew is a pretty, daisy-flowered perennial that has been used in herbal medicine for hundreds of years. Monks used to mix Feverfew concoctions with liberal doses of wine and honey to cure "them that are giddie in the head" or "such as be melancholike," but frankly, these inebriating elixirs probably contributed further to light-headedness and only temporarily lifted depression. This flower has also been used in poultices to treat bruises, and in distillations to clear freckles. In his book of herbal remedies that became so popular in the colonies, Nicholas Culpeper noted a particularly arcane use for Feverfew as "an especial remedy against opium taken too liberally."

Today, even though opium has been supplanted by other chemicals, Feverfew remains a desirable plant. It comes from a large genus that is often known for its enormous flowers, but this dainty little chrysanthemum is far from showy and will never be found on a cheerleader's sweater. *C. parthenium* is a lush, leafy plant often present in English cottage gardens, though some fancier gardeners disdain it as rather common. Margery Fish, who gardened in Somerset, England, and cherished her "old favorites," came to Feverfew's defense on this count, praising cottagers for "realizing the value of the plant when everyone else scorns it . . . it is one of those simple, attractive plants that grows as if it enjoyed it."

Feverfew grows up to two feet (60 cm) tall, producing plenty of small white and yellow flowers to last throughout the summer. *C. parthenium* is a prolific self-sower. Babies should appear all during the season—which is the *real* reason to grow this plant. Feverfew seedlings make wonderful hole-fillers for gardeners who anguish over Empty Spots. ("I wish you could have been here last week . . ." must be the most common garden tour introduction.) Instead of mourning over what has passed, simply transplant a Feverfew seedling and enjoy its old-fashioned, sweet-faced abundance. As Culpeper wrote: "It doth all the good you can desire from an herb."

Feverfew has been in gardens for centuries and makes a perfect gap filler in the modern border. In this English garden, Feverfew and Meconopsis cambrica *seed themselves happily year after year,* OPPOSITE. *Feverfew in Newfoundland,* BELOW.

Compositae

FEVERFEW

Corydalis lutea Fumariaceae

Perhaps because Yellow Corydalis has been in cultivation in England at least since 1596, and as it is just about one hundred percent reliable, many gardeners tend to dismiss this sweet plant as "that old thing." But Margery Fish loved the fumitories and devoted a whole chapter to them in her book *Cottage Garden Flowers* (1961). The yellow *Corydalis lutea* was her special favorite, and about it she wrote: "This plant has so many things to recommend it that I never understand why we do not treat it better. It never stops . . . and the little yellow flowers are worth examining carefully."

E. A. Bowles obviously took time to study these flowers closely and decided that the Greek *korydalis* (crested lark) made reference to the resemblance of the spurred flowers to the lark's hind toenail, a reference so obscure it just may be true.

Mrs. Fish described several other members of the Fumitory Family, but her heart remained true to the yellow. She said the white form "grows rather floppily" and that it

The cellar stairs at this English house sport a lovely clump of Yellow Fumitory. This plant takes well to North American conditions and will flower all summer if in a shaded spot. This flower self-seeds successfully.

and the pale lilac *Corydalis cava* are not "first-class plants." This *C. cava* is probably the fumitory that Culpeper recommended for treatment and prevention of "Saturnine diseases," and the name, *"cava,"* recalls the plant's hollow bulb, from which the narcotic and sedative alkaloids corydaline and bulbocapnine are obtained. An ethereal, blue flowering species, *Corydalis cashmeriana* sounds immediately tempting until one reads Fish's scathing description of this "lovely, expensive, and temperamental" member of the family: "It looks right through you, and then, having established relations, it decides it does not like you much after all and goes off to its plant heaven."

So, after having met the rest of the clan, *C. lutea* seems the sister with whom to make a commitment. It is a hardy perennial whose soft, fern-like foliage makes a mound about one foot (30 cm) high. In moderate climates this plant is evergreen, but severe weather may cause Corydalis to disappear for a while and take a winter break. Pretty yellow flowers appear in late spring, and if in a partially shaded position, *C. lutea* will flower almost continuously until autumn.

Graham Stuart Thomas is another famous gardener who admits to liking Yellow Fumitories, which he describes as "garden toys of great charm" and laments that they are "sometimes called common or trivial plants." When this excellent character reference is added to the role of *C. lutea* as the reliable sister, Yellow Fumitory establishes itself as a very desirable plant indeed. It is pretty, unlikely to desert, and, being a prolific seeder, will quickly produce a large family of little luteas for enjoyment in the gardener's old age.

Crambe cordifolia Cruciferae

A corruption of the name Colewort gave rise to the word collards—a vegetable rarely mentioned in conjunction with the finer things in life. Though proclaimed "King of the Cabbage Family," Colewort is one of those plants whose family does tend to let the side down a bit.

But one glance at a fine display of *Crambe cordifolia,* and all thoughts of odoriferous vegetables disappear. E. A. Bowles delighted in growing it right next to his house where, for over twenty years, it made "one huge cloud every June, about five feet square (only, like other clouds, it is round) of myriads of white flowers."

Crambe is Greek for "sea kale" and *cordifolia* refers to the lovely heart-shaped leaves. A relative, *C. maritima,* actually known as Sea Kale, is native to maritime sands in western Europe and in Devon. This plant has been cultivated for centuries, its early shoots blanched and eaten as succulent vegetables. But although Sea Kale is beautiful,

Penelope Hobhouse uses Crambe along one of the lovely borders at Tintinhull House in Somerset, England. The plant produces clouds of tiny flowers for weeks.

the only species generally deemed worthy of the flower garden is *C. cordifolia,* Colewort or Flowering Sea Kale, which came into ornamental gardens from the wilds of the Caucasus in 1822.

Flowering is truly the operative word here, as this Crambe produces the huge snowy clouds of blossom that so delighted Mr. Bowles. This is definitely a plant for the larger garden, as its handsome, wavy-edged, dark green leaves may grow almost three feet tall and can spread up to six feet (2m). The plant is very deep-rooted, so although the many branched panicles can reach as high as six feet, there is no need for staking. Besides, the giant Baby's-Breath effect is further enhanced if it is allowed room to billow and sprawl. The only maintenance that should not be ignored is cutting down the old foliage and flowering stems when they turn yellow. Although Colewort flowers have a distinctive smell when fresh, if any plant parts are allowed to rot, this plant will soon remind the lazy gardener of its family background.

Colewort is pretty in the large herbaceous border, alone in the wild garden, and, when planted in islands on the lawn, makes a blessed change from the dreaded Pampas Grass. Or, one may plant it next to the house as E. A. Bowles did and instruct garden visitors as he did seventy-five years ago: "Before we leave the doorstep, please pay a tribute of admiration to *Crambe cordifolia,* not only for its beauty, but also for its good nature."

Full warning should be given to the inexperienced gardener that dalliance with dianthus is likely to become habit-forming. These showy, delightfully fragrant flowers have long been the favorite of everyone from kings to weavers; their hardiness and ease of propagation have led many otherwise normal people down the long road to lifelong plant passion. But, given the choices—real estate gambling, aerobics, or television—dianthus addiction seems a delight-

(*dios,* divine, and *anthos,* flower). It was also probably the Coronary Flower used to crown heroes in ancient times, and one of the old clove pinks wildly popular at various periods in English history. (However, just to add to confusion, William Robinson notes that *Dianthus plumarius* was also sometimes called Clove Pink.)

By the middle of the 1500s, *D. caryophyllus* was parent to many garden varieties. A sixteenth-century

Dianthus Caryophyllaceae

fully fresh direction for twentieth-century compulsives.

The genus has a flower for every climate and every taste. Gerard wrote: "A great and large volume would not suffice to write of every one at large, in particular considering how infinite they are, and how every yeare, everye clymate and countrey bringth forth new sorts, and such as have not heretofore bin written of." But as this is not a great and large volume, a rather arbitrary selection from the genus, representing An Introduction, The Thin End of the Wedge, and The Blooming of Passion, will tell a very abbreviated story of the enticements of dianthus.

Today it is generally agreed that *Dianthus caryophyllus,* parent of the modern Carnation, was the flower the Greeks called the Divine Flower

Dianthus barbatus
SWEET WILLIAM
Dianthus deltoides
MAIDEN PINK
Dianthus plumarius
COTTAGE PINK

❧

Sweet William is an easy-to-grow spring delight from the ancient genus Dianthus. *Gerard noted that they were especially enjoyed in Elizabethan England, and here they shine during a rainy spring at Hatfield House,* LEFT *and* ABOVE. *The gardens at Hatfield are notable for their Dianthus collections, with some varieties having been collected in the early 1600s.*

writer, William Turner, remarked that "they have been made pleasant and sweet by the wit of Man and not by Nature." Largely because uninspired modern florists use carnations in the most dreadful creations ever to be called flower arrangements, it is very difficult to whip up enthusiasm even for the smaller-flowered Border Carnations. Somehow *D. caryophyllus* just seems too difficult to grow and too common a sight to get passionate over.

Although Sweet William could also be called a common sight, it has the charm and easiness that characterizes the best of this genus and will here serve as An Introduction to the pleasures of dianthus. Sweet William, *Dianthus barbatus,* is one of the most widely known species. It was given its common name many years ago when florists divided the broad-leafed bearded pinks from the narrow-leafed. The latter was christened Sweet John and promptly disappeared from cultivation, but Sweet William's fragrant, chintz-like flower remains a favorite to this day.

Most books give a date of 1573 for cultivation of the flower, but since there are also references to massive plantings of *D. barbatus* for Henry VIII in 1533 at Hampton Court, it seems that they earn a date fully forty years earlier. Thomas Jefferson grew Sweet Williams and noted their opening on April 16, 1767, at Shadwell, his birthplace.

The clusters of flowers are surrounded by a bush of greenery like a tiny stiff beard, but the name *barbatus,* meaning bearded, actually refers to the hairs on the petals. Flowers are usually single, but a famous double form, the dark crimson 'King Willie,' was bred in 1770 in a Scottish nursery. One turn-of-the-century book (*Garden Flowers* by Robert McCurdy) recommended that the gardener "go for the clear pink, white or crimson" and fussed that "the parti-colored ones are ugly and undesirable." Today, the gardener recognizes that many of the latter group have a wild charm of their own. The auricula-eyed Sweet William is very popular and devotees of this group claim that they have the sweetest scent of all.

Sweet Williams are good for beginners because they are very easy to grow. They are either biennial or perennial, depending upon whom

D. deltoides, *the Maiden Pink,* A B O V E, *is a brightly colored, sweetly scented member of the genus and is very easy to grow. Its narrow leaves often have a purple tinge, and it is excellent for growing between paving stones.*

one reads, but this really isn't an issue because they self-seed like mad. Buying plants assures a first season show and trusses of flowers up to four inches (10 cm) across will open anywhere from April in warm climates up until July and August during a mild northern summer. Keep most of the dead flowers cut off (this will have to be done with delicate scissors, not secateurs) but leave a few to make seeds.

Those who wonder how the widely known, easily grown Sweet William could possibly mark the beginning of a passion should read the description written by Gerard. Over

three hundred years ago he wrote that they were "kept and sustained in gardens more for to please the eye than either the nose or belly. They are not used either in meat or medicine, but esteemed for their beauty to deck up gardens, the bosoms of the beautiful, and garlands and crowns for pleasure."

Once one has had a great Sweet William success, decking gardens, bosoms, and crowns with this appealing little dianthus, it will be very difficult to resist the bright charms of the Maiden Pink. Although not nearly as easy to find as the introductory member, *Dianthus deltoides* is a cinch to grow, has a more characteristically dianthus-like appearance, and will quickly act as The Thin End of the Wedge. This little native of Britain grows in soft tufts of deep green foliage that is sometimes tinted purple or reddish. Like all other members of the genus, Maiden Pink likes well-drained soil and a bit of lime but can also thrive in partial shade. In fact, this dainty thing is hardy in America from New Hampshire to Georgia and makes such a wonderful burst of color in June and July that it is a wonder it is not more widely grown.

Although little written about, Maiden Pink is sweetly scented and makes a brilliant crevice filler. The flowers are small, usually well under an inch (2.5 cm) across, but their deep pink, red, or clear white color makes them irresistible for miniature bouquets. The Maiden Pink is a free-seeder and a free-pleaser, so

even the most wary of gardeners soon finds herself or himself wondering if it would really be possible to consider growing a few more dianthus . . . possibly one of the slightly larger-flowered. . . .

Once pinks have wedged their way into your garden, there is no turning back. The growing of *Dianthus plumarius* will certainly mark The Blooming of Passion.

D. plumarius is the Cottage Pink, native of Europe, and parent of the modern pinks. It has been grown for hundreds of years in English gardens, from grand to humble, and has inspired the type of love and devotion that a human being should only be too lucky to experience in a lifetime. This reliable, fragrant, hardy perennial may have taken its common name from the German *Pinksten* (Pentecost) and, eventually, gave it to that wonderful color which Miss Schiaparelli found so shocking.

The full Bloom of Pink Passion has been felt by many at many different periods, but probably one of

the most famous frenzies occurred in 1785 in Paisley, Scotland. In a town famous for shawls and strict nonconformity to the established church, the weavers began to put tremendous energy into breeding Laced Pinks. These passionate and skilled men eventually bred more than eighty new varieties from *plumarius,* which they proudly exhibited during their elaborate Annual and Amicable Competitions. As is often the case, this fervor waxed and then waned. Today, though, aside from a few varieties of Laced Pinks that were rescued and are still in cultivation,

~

D. plumarius, *Cottage Pink,* TOP RIGHT, *here growing at Hatfield, has inspired the passions of many for centuries. Breeding has produced a larger-flowered offspring, the Mule Pink,* BELOW, *as well as the famous Allwood strain,* TOP LEFT. D. plumarius *is evergreen in mild climates.*

many of the weavers' Laced Pinks exist only as a romantic story.

But not all passion ends in just memories. The most famous of all pinks was named for Catherine Sinkins by her husband. He worked as keeper of one of the most dreaded institutions of the last century, the workhouse. But obviously he had time for more pleasant pursuits, because the double white 'Mrs. Sinkins' was bred around 1870 and was later sold to Charles Turner, a nurseryman in Slough, England, who made it famous. Today the armorial bearings of Slough sport a swan holding a 'Mrs. Sinkins' in its beak.

Although there is much, much more to read about dianthus, it is probably best to grow a few first before plunging into a study of the genus. Then the pleasure of pretty dianthus faces, tufts of foliage, and sweet perfumes will make it easy to give in to devotion. As the respected artist, author and gardener Graham Stuart Thomas wrote about dianthus: "Who would have a garden without their fragrant flowers?"

BLEEDING-HEART *Dicentra spectabilis*

Before Queen Victoria's reign, English gardens, like those in the rest of the western world, suffered an annual affliction called the Dull Period. Beginning with the falling of autumn leaves and stretching interminably until the heartening appearance of the first snowdrops, the Dull Period offered the gardener little beyond evergreens for color and excitement. Robert Fortune, who was seven years old at the time of Victoria's accession, would later grasp the Dull Period by its boring neck and shake it into horticultural oblivion.

By the middle of Victoria's reign, England had explored or colonized all the corners of the world. The Royal Horticultural Society hired botanical explorers to search remote, often hostile, countries for plants that would brighten Britain's dreary winter. Robert Fortune was one such explorer. Before he left the comforts of home, he asked his employers to secure him permission to buy a gun. Although the East could often be quite unfriendly to visitors at this time, the London-based Royal Horticultural Society committee decided that Fortune's efforts would be better spent learning to speak Chinese. This he somehow never got around to, which makes his years of travel in China—sometimes disguised as a homeless Chinese beggar—even more remarkable.

His trips were very successful, as the many plants named *fortunei* testify. He gave western gardens Japanese anemones and chrysanthemums for autumn, winter-flowering honeysuckles and Winter Jasmine to cheer mild winters, and forsythia and *Dicentra spectabilis* for a bright spring. It was Dicentra that became well known as the finest hardy plant of that century and quickly became a must in many gardens.

Dicentra spectabilis had actually been discovered in Siberia as early as 1810, but the specimens did not survive in cultivation. In 1846, on a trip to the Japanese island of Chusan, while climbing mountain trails festooned with wild wisteria, Fortune rediscovered that most Victorian of plants, Bleeding-Heart.

Linnaeus had earlier named the plant *Dielytra* after its two-sheathed flower, but he had had the opportunity to examine only dried specimens. This is a pity, because there is nothing more charming and fresh than the long racemes of little pink hearts that gave the plant its common name. Other folk names include Lady's Locket and Lyre Flower, and if the little lyre-shaped petals are pulled back, a tiny white Lady-in-the-Bath will be revealed.

Some may consider the softer colors and increased hardiness of the American natives *D. eximia* ("choice") and *D. formosa* ("handsome") to be a plus, but for true Victorian whimsy, nothing beats Fortune's *spectabilis* ("remarkable").

Bleeding-Heart grows about two feet (60 cm) tall and creates an early, colorful mound of green in gardens showing predominantly bare soil. In April and May, it will send up racemes of pink and white flowers. It thrives when located in a sheltered spot that will protect it from late spring frosts and it prefers warm, light, rich soil. Dicentra doesn't mind the shade a bit. Because the leaves die back after flowering, plant Bleeding-Heart with blue Browallia or Christmas Fern to cover the empty spaces as the season progresses.

Bleeding-Heart makes a graceful addition to springtime flower arrangements and, if desired, can be dug up from its garden spot in autumn and forced to flower indoors very early in the season. There, while the days are still cold and terrible, pick a little heart and, in memory of Robert Fortune, bend its wings back to form a tiny pink Chinese sailing junk.

Fumariaceae

Both the pink and white forms of Dicentra flourish at Wave Hill, a public garden owned by New York City and located on the Hudson River in the Bronx.

Digitalis

FOXGLOVE

The common name for this well-loved English standby is from the Old English *Foxes glofa,* and most people think the image of foxes with petal gloves is a fitting one. But the irregular spelling habits of ancient scribes have led some floral historians to write that the name is really a corruption of Folks' Glove and refers to the Little Folks or fairies. For people who welcome compromise, there is yet another story—that naughty Little Folks gave the flowers to foxes so that they might better sneak up on the chicken coop. Whether a paw or a tiny hand wears the glove, *Digitalis* is named for the fingerlike shape of the corolla.

Foxglove is famous for being the source of digitalis, a life-saving drug for heart patients, and, from the comfort of hindsight, it seems curious that neither Gerard nor Culpeper had a clue about using the plant for cardiac ailments. (Culpeper said only that he was "confident that an ointment of it is one of the best remedies for a scabby head that is.") It was not until 1785 that English physician William Withering began to investigate the custom of giving leaves of the plant to those suffering edema, and only in the beginning of the nineteenth century was its full worth officially noted.

Since there is no synthetic source for digitalis, fields of *Digitalis purpurea* and *Digitalis lanata* are still raised

Although the stately Foxglove has been a garden favorite for centuries, its lifesaving potential was not realized until the early 1800s. Digitalis at Chelsea Physic Garden in London, OPPOSITE, *and in a shady palm garden,* ABOVE.

purpurea scrophulariaceae

for pharmacological use. The leaves of the darker-flowered plants produce the best medicine, so during the second year of the plant, just as the flowers appear (when it can be ascertained which plants have the deepest-colored buds), the leaves are harvested and a "wonder drug" begins in a most natural way.

Several kinds of foxglove are recommended for garden use. *Digitalis grandiflora* was brought from Greece in 1596. As Graham Stuart Thomas rather cryptically writes, "It is a pleasing, short, clump forming perennial in creamy yellow—need I say more?" *Digitalis lutea* is a graceful foxglove with tiny, yellowish flowers that would fit only the littlest Little Folk. Either of these are pretty in the garden, but several modern forms of *D. purpurea* should be cautioned against: those ungraceful plants with flowers around the stem, and those called 'Gloxiniiflora' whose wide-open flowers resemble those of Gloxinia.

Digitalis purpurea is the old favorite native to Great Britain, and has the colors and form to make it a wonderful garden plant. It is the Foxglove mentioned in the *Feate of Gardening* written by the aptly named John Gardener in 1440, and it is common to see *D. purpurea* in white, cream, rose, or maroon.

White Foxgloves look particularly romantic and were favored in many antique garden books. One writer waxed eloquent and urged the naturalistic gardener to plant "spires of white Foxglove so that they ascend at the half-shaded entrance to woodland cathedral aisles," and for those with wooded areas, this poetic advice is hard to ignore.

❧

Digitalis purpurea, OPPOSITE *and* TOP LEFT, *is native to Great Britain.* D. grandiflora, TOP RIGHT, *arrived from Greece by 1596, and* D. lutea, BOTTOM, *is from Italy. All are easy to grow and thrive in fertile, shady areas.*

Richardson Wright once mournfully wrote that "the shady border is among the least of God's mercies," but he certainly was forgetting about Foxgloves when he made that complaint. They are a blessing for narrow borders where hollyhocks and delphiniums would be impossible, and their free-seeding natures soon lead them to decide on their own where else they might like to be. They look very pretty in front of dark shrubs such as rhododendrons, and, for those lucky enough to have garden walls, Foxgloves will grow along the top and make marvelous garden sentinels.

If there are pets prone to leaf-chewing in the garden, a warning is in order. Rover should be told that a lesser-known name for Foxglove is Dead Man's Bells and that restraint from snacking is essential. Otherwise, he is very likely to find himself in a little grave in that woodland cathedral, with perhaps some white Foxgloves planted overhead.

Dipsacus fullonum Dipsacaceae

There is much to be said about gardens in wintertime and the need to plant shrubs with interesting bark or intriguing forms that create nice effects against the snow. But one also has to keep in mind that the summer forms of these shrubs can be something less than beautiful. Blood-red twigs of Tartarian Dogwood are pretty against a bright blue winter sky, but enduring the large, lumpish shrubs the rest of the year is a test of good will. Contorted Hazel is unspeakably ugly with its leaves on, and many hollies are impossible for a small garden. The real problem with these plants is that they must be planted near windows so that they can be seen and enjoyed in their midwinter prime, and thus, one is forced to deal with them quite intimately all the other months of the year.

One way to circumvent this dilemma is to use herbaceous plants that are pretty in summer and leave interesting skeletons for the winter months. A particularly good example is the tall, dynamic Teasel. Although inappropriate for a formal garden, Teasel's pale purple flowers look wonderful against a wooden fence in the autumn. Later, in the dead of winter, bleached stems with brown cones will stand stalwart through the trials and tribulations of fierce weather and cast long, lonely shadows on the snow.

Teasel, here pictured at the Memorial University Botanic Garden in Newfoundland, is an easy plant for informal gardens. Growing four to six feet tall, it is useful for creating vertical interest in the wild garden and will stand tall during harsh winter gales and snows.

Wild Teasel, also called Gypsy Combs, is common along roadsides and wastelands in Europe and England and has naturalized in America from Maine to Virginia. Culpeper was so sure of his readers' familiarity with the plant that he wrote in his *Herball* that it required no description. He gave his catch-all medicinal pitch for the plant: cure for warts, worms, and womanly distresses. He also mentioned that Wild Teasel has small, soft, and upright prickles as opposed to Fuller's Teasel, which has stiff, hooked prickles.

Many old books call *D. fullonum* Fuller's Teasel, and an old issue of the *Cottage Gardener* describes how to harvest the heads for combing wool. But *Hortus Third* absolutely disagrees with all the rest and firmly states that Fuller's Teasel, with hooked tips, is *D. sativus*. It might be disappointing to those who enjoy useful plants to learn that their *D. fullonum* can't be employed to tease wool, but, unless someone has the nerve to challenge the L. H. Bailey Hortorium, *D. fullonum* is not the teasel grown by fullers. This fairly useless gardening information is the sort of obscure knowledge that is wonderful to have and flaunt.

The prickly branching stem of this biennial will quickly grow four to six feet (2 m) tall, producing dark green leaves with a strong, white midrib. William Robinson (1838-1935), outspoken advocate of the natural garden, noted the fine foliage and habit of the plant makes "a good effect" in informal garden areas. Pale purple flowers that appear in late summer or autumn have a charming way of blooming in colorful bands around the cylindrical head. *D. fullonum* is very easy to raise by seed, has no special cultural requirements, and thus could make quite a striking addition to the well-planned meadow garden.

But don't forget its winter purpose. Plant at least one where it will be visible from warm interiors. The strong form, silvered like driftwood, will stand like a delicate sculpture in the bare garden and will remind one of that champion of weeds Margery Fish. She was especially fond of Teasel in February and wrote that "there are many times when I am glad of its company."

Eremurus robustus Liliaceae

Eremurus robustus is one of those plants that truly deserves the respect of its full botanical name. It was brought into European gardens from Turkestan in 1874. Although it looks incredibly exotic, it is reliably hardy and has been known to push up shoots through frozen soil. Once Eremurus starts pushing, one should be warned to stand back. This big boy of the Lily Family produces leaves four feet (over a meter) long and, eventually, a huge flower spike that waves eight to ten feet (3 m) above the earth. This flower was not named *robustus* as a joke.

E. robustus is one of two things: either "JUST too big!" or "JUST must have!" If feelings fall into the latter category, the would-be purchaser must be warned that this is not an especially easy plant to locate and that one must insist upon healthy, three-year-old specimens. Eremurus is an expensive treat, and there is nothing worse than suffering a costly disappointment.

Once the sought-after tuberous

This giant of the Lily family is sure to excite the most jaded gardener. Pictured here at Hatfield, it grows equally well in America.

roots are obtained, one may wonder how such huge plants grow from such odd looking objects. Have faith and plant the octopus-shaped roots in deep, rich, sandy loam. Do not overcrowd the roots and don't bother to plant them in the first place unless there is plenty of sunshine and good drainage in the desired location. *E. robustus* is not amused about being moved and will likely just up and die an expensive death if disturbed. Decide where to plant it and leave it alone.

Eremurus rewards the gardener for these troubles. Early in the season, long straps of leaves start filling up the empty border. (These are welcome, though one should be prepared for them to disappear later.) The real show begins around June, when a spike appears and begins to

grow like Jack's beanstalk. At about eight feet (2.4 m) high, it produces a dense raceme, nearly four inches (10 cm) in diameter, of pretty flowers. The flowers have been described as "peach-shaded lilac," "silvery-rose," or "coppery," with the disparity obviously caused by the fact that it's very difficult to get high enough to look at the things closely.

But—the flower racemes are beautiful. They are wonderful. They are arresting. They are fragrant. And since they may last for weeks, one has plenty of time to show off the magnificent display. Even if one's most admired garden friend is on vacation and misses the best-ever Eremurus show, the blossoms are followed by seed pods, so evidence of an incredible green thumb remains long after the June flowering. Then, if the admired garden friend is sufficiently apologetic about having been in France while the flowering splendor was at home, you can always promise him or her a few new crowns next year.

Although weird-looking to the point of artificiality, *Fritillaria meleagris* is so dainty and graceful that its strange appearance is beautiful rather than alarming. Appearing as modern as a punk ballerina in a plaid tutu, Checkered Lily actually has been in cultivation for centuries. As Alice Morse Earle wrote in 1901: "In no garden, no matter how modern, could the fritillaries ever look to me aught but antique and classic."

Most sources agree that Checkered Lily is a native of Great Britain, where it was given odd folk names implying an unsavory reputation. (Sullen Lady and Madam Ugly are among its nicknames.) Perhaps old cottagers found the tessellation of the petals too fancy or the drooping head too viperish (another name is Snake's-Head), but nevertheless, they carried on growing Fritillaries like mad, which just goes to prove that a Fritillary by any other name is still a charming flower.

Gerard was fascinated with *F. meleagris* and carefully described its squares of color, adding that "every leafe seems to be the feather of a Ginnie hen, whereof it took its name"—the Guinea-Hen Flower. Its botanical name is from *meleagris,* meaning speckled, and *fritillus,* a dice cup.

There are other interesting members of the genus including *Fritillaria pudica,* a native of the American West Coast which, thanks to the turn-of-the-nineteenth-century wilderness explorations of Lewis and Clark, found its way back to Monti-

CHECKERED LILY

GUINEA-HEN FLOWER

SNAKE'S-HEAD

Fritillaria meleagris Liliaceae

cello in Virginia. Thomas Jefferson had persuaded Congress to finance the western explorations, and his nurseryman friend Bernard Mc-Mahon was curator of the Lewis and Clark plant collection. One wonders, though, if Jefferson was ever as thrilled with *pudica* as he was with another more imposing member of the genus, *Fritillaria imperialis,* Crown Imperial.

Crown Imperials are taller and showier in spring beds than the loftiest and most brightly colored Tulips. For this reason alone, one may love or hate them. They are one of the oldest known cultivated plants. Dutch painters loved to include them in their floral extravaganzas. However, anyone who has ever been in close range of the flower wonders how the artists could work with such a terrible odor wafting from their large bells. Perhaps they were simply ready to sacrifice all for art.

But as loud and brash as a bed of

Dainty Checkered Lilies, OPPOSITE *and* TOP LEFT, *are delightful in the spring garden, and this magical little flower should be planted especially for children.* F. persica, BELOW, *is darker and less graceful, and* F. imperialis, TOP RIGHT, *may smell unpleasant.*

Crown Imperials can be, there is nothing more sweet and delightful than a patch of unmown spring grass, filled with the drooping bells of Checkered Lily. Blooming from April through May, these flowers love a moist, humus-rich soil in semishade, and will increase if happy. Simply dig them up in autumn, dislodge the offsets and replant. Do not leave the bulbs lying about, as gnawing pets may suffer quite severe stomachaches from snacking on them.

In her book about old-fashioned flowers, Lys de Bray gives excellent advice about planting fritillaries: never plant just one. "Go without something inessential like new saucepans, or a holiday, and put the cats on a starvation diet (which will encourage them to stir themselves to catch mice) but never plant one of anything." At the very least, plant enough *F. meleagris* to have a full performance of plaid-clad ballerinas.

Gladiolus byzantinus Iridaceae

SWORD LILY

Graham Stuart Thomas makes no bones about his views on gladioli: "The size and vulgarity of the large flowered hybrids are only surpassed by the very large flowered dahlias and chrysanthemums. On the other hand, there are [old gladioli] that are dainty and charming." He continues by describing the graceful, magenta-flowered *Gladiolus byzantinus* as tops among the dainty and charming contingent.

Most Americans would never think of putting gladioli in an old-fashioned garden, but genus *Gladiolus* is surprisingly ancient. Several species were grown by Gerard, and *G. byzantinus,* a traveler from Turkey, was firmly established in Parkinson's garden by 1629. Because *G. byzantinus* is fairly common in the eastern Mediterranean region, some garden historians feel that this is the flower that Ovid described as springing from the spilt blood of

The lovely Sword Lily in Margery Fish's garden, OPPOSITE, *with old-fashioned* Geranium endressii. ABOVE, *A profusion of Sword Lilies growing in a private garden in Somerset, England.*

Hyacinthus. As sometimes happens, these historians take their case to the *n*th degree by claiming that the white marks on the flower's petals are the hieroglyphics for "AI, AI," the dying man's last call.

There being no eyewitnesses to that final testimony, take it as legend. But do take as fact that *G. byzantinus* is hardier than most gladioli and is known to survive without autumn lifting in Britain and the southern United States. "Treat like gladiolus," however, is catalogese for "take up the tuber or corm in question before frost." Gardeners in

colder areas will need to experiment with hardiness, but there is nothing simpler or more pleasant than digging corms (as the gladiolus's underground stem is known) on a crisp autumn day, with a view to safely storing them during the cold winter.

Gladiolus byzantinus likes warm, dry soil and a sunny, open exposure. It looks pretty in the wild garden, in open woods, or standing proudly in front of dark green shrubbery. It also mixes well with other border plants, and is especially pretty with blue flowers like Baptisia. Unlike its cossetted modern grandchildren—who can be called strong-headed but weak-willed—*G. byzantinus* has no need for staking.

In the Victorian language of flowers, gladioli stood for a strong character. *Gladiolus byzantinus* represents all the positive aspects of that attribute without the "vulgarity" so abhorred by Mr. Thomas.

Hesperis matronalis Cruciferae

SWEET ROCKET
DAME'S ROCKET
DAME'S VIOLET

The beautifully named, night-scented Hesperis is native to hedges and bushy areas in central and southern Europe. Long a favorite of the French, this plant probably made its way to England during the persecution of the Huguenots.

In his book *The Coming of the Flowers,* A.W. Anderson wrote about the dissolution of the English monasteries in the early sixteenth century and the disastrous effect upon culture in general and horticulture specifically that upheaval had. He credits the influx of the Huguenots into England with partial responsibility for reviving gardening skills among the ordinary population, and describes the influence these middle-class merchants, lacemakers, gardeners, and weavers had upon their new homeland: "A quiet and industrious people, they soon began to establish their own ways of life in the new land, and brought a skill for gardening and a love for individual flowers that was hitherto unknown outside their own country. . . . It is pleasant to think that Rocket and Honesty have remained essentially the same as in the days when they were smuggled across the English Channel."

Parkinson knew Rocket and noted that its "pretty sweet scent" is almost totally absent during the day. It was also once known as Queen Gillyflower because it was superior to all the other gillyflowers, which in those days included famed perfumers such as stocks, Wallflowers, and pinks. The sweet, spicy perfume of this plant is quite desirable for those who especially enjoy their gardens at night.

The single form of Rocket is not difficult to cultivate, with evidence of its compliance apparent in areas of America and Great Britain where it has happily naturalized. In the garden it will grow about two to three feet (one meter) tall with rough, toothed leaves, and will make eighteen-inch (45-cm) spikes of white, mauve, or purple flowers that open in June. The flowers resemble those of its relative, Honesty, and like that plant it will form clumps that may continue blooming until August.

Beautifully scented Sweet Rocket was a sentimental favorite of Huguenots fleeing from Europe to Britain in the late 1500s. The single form, photographed here at Hatfield, is very simple to grow and will tolerate half-shade.

Also like Honesty, there is some discussion as to whether the plant is biennial or perennial, so it is best to sow seeds every year to insure a continuous crop.

A more difficult, but frankly more beautiful form of the plant is the Double Rocket. This plant, a favorite of Marie Antoinette, is said to be "highly temperamental, difficult at best" and demands that chalk be added to its soil. Then, having supped of this favored food for a

Another view of Hesperis at Hatfield, here planted in a bed near roses and irises. This plant, which releases its perfume at night, seeds freely and is not particular about soil.

while, it will quickly tire of its locale to such a degree that Double Rocket will quietly die of starvation, boredom, or whatever it is that kills off these lovely plants with maddening regularity. Some gardeners transplant their precious Double Rocket every other year and swear that this is the way to keep the plant interested in life. The only sure way to propagate Double Rocket is by taking cuttings of nonflowering shoots and over-wintering in the same way

as with Wallflowers.

But if Double Rocket is impossible to work into one's gardening routine, the single form constitutes a very nice consolation prize indeed. The perfect commuter's flower, there could be no better way to unwind from a long day's work than to sit in the garden and enjoy Hesperus, the evening star, and Hesperis, the evening scent, in sweet simultaneity.

New crops of Sweet Rocket should be raised about every three years to prevent woody roots and reduced flower production. Colors may range from lilac to white. The double form, LEFT, is very temperamental, and this clump receives careful cossetting at Margery Fish's restored garden.

CANDYTUFT

These little flowers are so delightful in every way that the name Candytuft seems to refer to some wonderful old-fashioned confection. This is not the case, however, but is instead a salute to Candia, another name for Crete. Annual Candytuft, *Iberis umbellata,* comes in all shades of pink, rose, violet, and white and was in cultivation by 1596. *Iberis sempervirens,* the Perennial Candytuft, did not come along until the relatively late date of 1739, when it was sent to Chelsea Physic Garden to show off its white flowers.

Candytuft is a humble little flower, but an indispensably sweet note in every cottage garden. It doesn't seem to have inspired much comment except that seeds from the annual form were used in cooking instead of mustard. Parkinson haughtily dismissed the plant saying "Candie, or Spanish tufts, is not so sharp biting in taste . . . and therefore is not to be used in medicines," provoking one to wonder if medi-

cines were formerly judged more effective if they tasted awful. Lys de Bray writes that one of the folk names for Candytuft is Billy-Come-Home-Soon, but the origin of the name is obscure. Perhaps it was planted along the garden paths that led wandering boys back to their own front door.

Both the annual and perennial forms of candytuft are small plants for the front of the border, for lining walks, or for rockeries. They quickly form showy masses that usually stay low and compact. The perennial is evergreen in mild climates, and both are considered strong growers that thrive in any soil. Iberis will tolerate a bit of shade, but prefers "to lie a-basking in the sun."

Every garden needs an occasional touch of the unostentatious. Iberis is just that and, as Robert McCurdy advised in 1917, "By all means have in your home garden a bit of candytuft whose blossoms are never melted by the sun."

Annual Candytuft is an unassuming little flower that was very popular in gardens a few generations ago. Native to hot climates, this sweet plant loves sun and heat. Pictured here during a drought at Monticello.

Iberis umbellata Cruciferae

Tiger Lily was grown only as a vegetable—in vast quantities in brown, muddy fields—in other words, about as romantic as hard work. Forget rich silk robes swishing past perfumed flower beds. Think field crops of onions.

Tiger Lilies were rescued from their rather ignominious position in China by Englishman William Kerr, the first professional collector to set up residence there. From 1803 until 1811, he was sponsored by Kew and the East India Company, and sent back *Kerria japonica, Lonicera japonica, Rosa banksiae,* and, in 1804, *Lilium lancifolium,* the Tiger Lily. Its orange-red flowers and strong constitution made it an instant favorite, and it quickly became an institution. At the beginning of the twentieth century, Western demand for any kind of lily bulbs was at a

During Marco Polo's visit to the native haunts of the Tiger Lily, he was amazed by the level of sophistication in Chinese ornamental gardening. Today it is easy to daydream about Tiger Lilies and see them as treasured pets that an Eastern prince would have been proud to show to his guest during a postprandial stroll around the royal grounds. But sometimes the truth is difficult.

Although the graceful Tiger Lily is one of the oldest lilies in cultivation, and although it has always been a very important plant in the East, there is very little chance that Kublai

Lilium lancifolium

These Tiger Lilies thrive in the short Newfoundland summer. Lance-leafed foliage makes a pretty garden feature.

Khan showed off his Tiger Lilies to his Venetian visitor. The modern equivalent of such an unlikely event would be the President of the United States leading the Italian ambassador around the White House Rose Garden and bragging about the potato crop growing there. In China the

peak. For example, in 1912, the Yokohama Nursery Company alone fulfilled orders for 15 million bulbs of beautiful *L. auratum,* Gold-banded Lily. On a wider scale, such a frenzy of lily growing was bound to encourage diseases, and it was soon realized that lily mosaic, a disease spread by aphids, was largely to blame for less than five percent flowering rate. Thus lilies gained their bad reputation as finicky.

There is bad news and good news about Tiger Lilies and mosaic virus. Bulbs of *L. lancifolium* are usually infected with mosaic, but for some reason, do not die from it as other lilies do. So, while it is unlikely that these flowers will fail, one does have to realize that the pride and joy of an autumn garden is in fact a vegetable form of Typhoid Mary. So for those who only want one kind of lily, the indestructible Tiger is tops.

Tiger Lilies are especially valuable in the garden because they are among the last lilies to bloom and they are simply just not fussy about soil or situation. Tiny black bulbils form in the leaf axils, fall from the sturdy stalk, and actually worm their way into the soil. Within two years these form new flowering-size bulbs. The plant grows two to five feet (60 cm to 1.5 m) tall and produces three

Liliaceae

to twelve flowers per stem, so one can quickly have a lovely mass of these fine flowers.

The placement of Tiger Lily is not to be taken lightly. First of all, once planted, they are unlikely to leave. Second, their color is not to be ignored. Russell Page, one of the best twentieth-century garden designers, had appealing ideas for where to grow this plant. In his autobiography, *The Education of a Gardener,*

TIGER LILY

Martagon Lilies make a wonderful display at Hatfield House in June. They are naturally resistant to lily mosaic.

⌇

Page wrote of the dream garden he would create if he only had the time. In a woodland planting removed from the house, he thought to plant Willow Gentian, False Solomon's Seal and Tiger Lilies—a lovely idea that should be executed by someone in memory of the great designer who made so many gardens for oth-

ers that he never was able to create his own.

Tiger Lilies are also ideal for naturalizing in the tall, unmown grass of meadow gardens. Left strictly alone for years on end, they will soon produce enough plants that one will be able to thrill the most horticulturally disinclined visitor. Give that jaded soul another jolt and serve him up a few bulbs with the roast. It will be worth his wonder, and who knows, he might even want a few Tiger Lilies for his own turf. Everyone knows that gardeners are born in the most unusual ways.

Lunaria annua Cruciferae

English poet Michael Drayton, a contemporary of Shakespeare's, wrote that "enchanting lunarie here lies in sorceries excelling" but he was probably referring to the mystical *Botrychium lunaria* or Moonwort Fern rather than Honesty. It was Moonwort Fern that reportedly made horses cast their shoes, whereas *Lunaria annua* had a more stable reputation as growing particularly well for those who relished telling the whole truth. Lunaria was generally considered by country people to be a helpful herb because, like all members of Cruciferae, it has cross-shaped flowers and, according to an old saying, "Health is in the Cross." Those who took these words literally, as most in those days did, often added the tasty roots to their salads.

Lunaria annua was brought into cultivation from Sweden in 1570, and other forms, white-flowered (1570), variegated (1894), and a perennial species, *Lunaria rediviva* (1596), are also pleasingly old. In 1597 Gerard wrote that a Swiss surgeon used Honesty for wounds and recommended it for treating epilepsy, leading one to wonder if there was an association between being moonstruck, the moon-like appearance of the dried plant, and its common name Moonwort.

Lunaria was a very early favorite in New World gardens. John Josselyn included it in his 1665 list of

HONESTY

MONEY PLANT

Honesty was very popular in England and New England centuries ago. American botanist Asa Gray said that the plant's common name came from the transparent pod, which renders the contents visible to all. The dried septums turn silver and are pretty in arrangements or left in the winter garden.

～

vegetables and flowers grown in the colonies. Very little would be known of this country's earliest gardens if it were not for the cheerful, matter-of-fact reporting of Josselyn in his *New England Rarities Discovered*. He called the plant White Satten, echoing Gerard's description of the pod as "like a piece of white sateen newly cut."

Another document that shows the early popularity of the plant in America is from a Boston newspaper published in 1760. In a seedman's advertisement listing over 100 different flowers, Honesty is the only plant annotated "to be sold in small parcels that everyone may have some." Later, American botanist Asa Gray (1810–1888) wrote that the name Honesty arose from the fact that the transparent pods made the contents entirely visible.

Although named *annua*, Honesty is often described as "a biennial with scentless violet flowers," or "a biennial with fragrant purple flowers." Thomas Jefferson wrote that it has "an indifferent flower," but many gardeners find its flowers pretty and useful in the border. Descriptive discrepancies abound in the garden, but there is no disagreement that the most charming characteristic of this plant is the satiny inner septums that look like pearly pennies. These are the currency of childhood fantasies and give the plant its folk-names: Money Flower, Money Seed, and Money-in-Both-Pockets.

Honesty grows about two to three feet (1 m) high and does well in a semishaded position. It looks especially nice on walls along with other free-seeders such as Snapdragons, Wallflowers, and Centranthus.

For those who positively dread the thought of dried flower arrangements gathering dust all winter, there is absolutely no law declaring that Honesty's famed silvery septums must be used in this manner. They have a wonderful ghostly beauty when left on their branches *in situ* in the winter garden, or they may be harvested like magical fruit and saved for celebrations. The dried satiny moons make a wonderful substitute for confetti and are perfectly symbolic for tossing over a newly-wedded bride and groom.

Lysimachia punctata Primulaceae

YELLOW LOOSESTRIFE

Yellow Loosestrife is a wonderful plant for boggy areas, but care must be taken to prevent rampant spreading. It has naturalized in America and Great Britain and is pictured here, TOP OPPOSITE, *in a private Newfoundland garden. It makes good color and form in difficult garden spots.*

⁓

Yellow Loosestrife is a brightly flowered plant found along English river and canal banks. Having long ago escaped from cottage gardens, Lysimachia is considered an invader by some and a lifesaver by others. Most say that *Lysimachia punctata* arrived in gardens in 1820, but one book published in 1846, *Johnson's Gardener's Dictionary and Cultural Instructor,* lists the much earlier date of 1658.

Lysimachia is a member of the Primrose Family and every garden book ever printed always warns to avoid confusing this plant with the Purple Loosestrife, *Lythrum salicaria.* They are two quite distinct and unrelated plants (which shows the usefulness of botanical nomenclature), but it should be said that Lysimachia stakes the best claim on the folk name because *lysis* means "dissolving" and *mache* translates as "strife."

The soothing qualities of this plant have been written about for centuries. Gerard claimed that the botanical name arose as a salute to King Lysimachus's discovery that a wreath of Yellow Loosestrife tied in the yoke of a pair of oxen would appease the surliness and unruliness of the beasts while plowing. Frankly, this story just does not hold water. It seems highly unlikely that royalty would be found plowing fields, but even if King Lysimachus did find this sort of manual labor a good way to work off a banquet or two, Alice Lounsberry wrote in *A Guide to Wild Flowers* (1899) that "unless the farmer has, in case of emergency, provided himself with such a wreath, we can imagine he would have some difficulty in guiding his fractious beasts to search for the plant by the brooks or wet meadows." Culpeper's use for the plant is much more believable and is one that calls for modern experimentation. "The smoke hereof being burned, driveth away flies and gnats, which in the night time molest people in marshes and fenny countries."

As can be assumed from its naturalized habitat, Lysimachia needs plenty of moisture and prefers a sunny position. It is a long-lived perennial that grows about three feet (1 m) tall and, in July and August, produces whorls of yellow cup-like flowers that nestle close to the stem. Yellow Loosestrife is just the plant to cheer up a difficult, wet area. It quickly creates a broad sweep of color, remains luxuriant for a long period of time, and, if the area tends to have mosquitoes, it just may keep them away. It is certainly worth giving this natural repellent a try.

Lythrum's position in the Scientific Hall of Fame was firmly established by Charles Darwin. When the eminent naturalist was working on the theory of the origin of species, he was intrigued by Lythrum's trimorphic flower. His experiments with it are interesting for those with a botanical background, but for the amateur gardener, let it suffice to say that Darwin's excitement over the plant was so intense that he wrote to his friend Dr. Gray: "I am almost stark, staring mad over lythrum. For the love of Heaven, have a look at some of your species, and, if you

they glow," (Neltje Blanchan in *Nature's Garden*) and, indeed, there is some concern about rampant spread of wild Lythrum. But the gardener may rest assured that cultivated forms do not set seed and don't contribute to this purple menace.

Given moist soil, Lythrum flowers prolifically in July and August and offers a pleasing contrast with the ubiquitous yellow flowers of high summer. It is a bit unfortunate that when the sun is at its glaring worst, most flowers in the garden also seem like bright spots of hot, hot colors. But Lythrum's rose,

Lythrum salicaria Lythraceae

PURPLE
LOOSESTRIFE

This hardy plant makes slender spikes of blooms late in July and August, and the foliage turns a soft golden in autumn. It is useful in the garden and in lovely old-fashioned arrangements.

⌒

can get me some seed, do!"

Lythrum is the Purple Loosestrife that all garden books warn NOT to confuse with Yellow Loosestrife, an issue we have already covered in the description of Lysimachia. Since Lythrum is quicker to say than Purple Loosestrife, the botanical name is probably better and less confusing.

The genus name arises from *lythron,* which means black blood and supposedly refers to the color of the flowers. Since Lythrum's flowers are a lovely rosy purple, one wonders if it was a colorblind person who was asked to name this plant. Culpeper says that Lythrum is good for all sorts of eye ailments, but obviously it didn't always work for that prob-

lem. The specific epithet, *salicaria,* means "like a willow" and may either refer to the willow-like leaves, the plant's choice of wet habitats, or the graceful form of the stalks.

Lythrum is an Old World native that has naturalized in America, "year by year extending its course of empire through low meadow marshes with torches that lengthen even as

pink, or magenta shades can inspire new summer schemes to include pink Cleomes, Queen Anne's Lace, and perhaps touches of deep blue Browallia. None of these flowers requires any work at all, and their colors are certainly perfect to enjoy while sipping an icy gin and tonic.

Then, when the heat of the summer is blessedly over, and the cool, clear blue skies of September and October once again make gardening a pleasure, Lythrum will cast a final trump card. As if to harmonize with the glowing reds, oranges, and browns of autumn, its leaves will turn a soft glowing yellow that lasts for weeks. So to paraphrase Darwin, if you can get some, do!

PLUME POPPY

The stately Plume Poppy was discovered in China in 1795, where its yellow sap had long been used as a dye and disinfectant. Perhaps its height, anywhere from six to ten feet (2 to 3 m), appealed to the Victorian love of curiosities, because it quickly became a garden rage. It was named in honor of Alexander Macleay, a Secretary of the Linnaean Society. One can only hope that Macleay was tall enough himself to avoid suffering a Napoleonic complex over his popular namesake.

Macleaya is a hardy herbaceous perennial that the venerable Sanders says "does well in suburban gardens." (Sanders's *The Flower Garden* was published in Great Britain in 1935 and ragged copies are still cherished by knowledgeable gardeners.) Another book reckons that Macleaya's long, branching stems and large leaves are perfect to "mask an untidy garden feature," so the clever modern gardener will quickly deduce that this is just the plant to hide the horrible garage next door.

One could not ask for a more beautiful screen. The crisply cut leaves are pale green, accented with

Plume Poppies grow at least ten feet tall in a Long Island garden.

Macleaya cordata Papaveraceae

reddish veins and stems, and the slightest breeze will catch them like kites, rustling them about with flashes of silvery undersides. This wonderful plant forms a root system so strong that, in spite of its height, it requires no staking.

Some books seem to confuse *Macleaya cordata* with *Macleaya microcarpa,* but the majority agree with *Hortus* that the former is the Plume Poppy. There is also disagreement as to the proper placement of the plant. Some call for a strong, back-of-the-border position, while others cry that since the foliage looks good from the ground up (unlike Hollyhock, for example) Macleaya should be given a relatively isolated position where it can multiply freely and "form bold groups." A plant ten feet tall could never make anything less than a bold statement, but a warning against its invasive nature should be taken to heart.

Macleaya does, of course, make flowers. But their tiny size, tan color, and lofty distance from the normal-sized viewer makes them hard to appreciate. Perhaps, however, H. H. Thomas was looking on the bright side when he wrote "Add to these recommendations the fact that it blooms in August, a month that is not distinguished by the opening of many fresh flowers, and it will be seen that here is a plant of no ordinary value." Macleaya is a valuable garden plant, but unless one wants to climb onto the garage roof to admire flowers, it should be grown solely for its outstanding leaves.

*Like most English gardens, this one has pretty
stands of Welsh Poppies to brighten difficult positions.
American gardeners should try these as an alternative to the nasturtium.*

Meconopsis

ambrica Papaveraceae

WELSH POPPY

The Welsh Poppy belongs to a small genus named for its resemblance to true poppies (*mekon,* a poppy, and *opsis,* resemblance). Although it appears fragile, this plant's reproductive rate inspired one garden writer to muse "It is quite irresponsible, yet it has great beauty and charm."

In 1640 Parkinson mentioned that *Meconopsis cambrica* grew "in many places" in Wales, and today the yellow Welsh Poppy seems to show up in just about every garden throughout the United Kingdom. Despite this popularity (or is it merely pervasiveness?), another meconopsis, *Meconopsis betonicifolia,* is the one most gardeners have read about. This is the famous Blue Poppy, first seen high in the Himalayas in 1886, and, years later, collected by the famous plant explorer Frank Kingdon-Ward. He later recalled the celestial beauty of that field of azure poppies and wrote that it was like "a blue panel dropped from Heaven." All this romance makes every gardener want to rush out and plant a field of *M. betonicifolia*—no difficult feat in the climate of Great Britain, but in the United States, this has got to be one of the most difficult plants to get to flower. And once it does, it promptly dies.

But where *M. betonicifolia* is fussy and elusive, *M. cambrica* is steadfast and cheerful. So when it comes to the genus *Meconopsis,* one has the choice of either mourning the disappearing act of the blue or of delighting in the productive hardiness of the yellow.

Welsh Poppy seeds may take a while to germinate, but once they do, the plant will thrive just about anywhere. Poor soil is no deterrent to its determined colonization, and pretty, clear yellow flowers will quickly sprout in the most unlikely places—chinks in walls, cracks in cement, even straight up through gravel paths.

The leaves of this plant are especially pretty, forming basal clumps of ferny foliage that are a pleasing mid-green in color. The long scape is erect and holds a single lemon-yellow flower with good floral posture that more plants should emulate. The flowers generally appear sporadically from June to September, with small poppy-like seed heads following. A good stock of Welsh Poppies is insured if these seed heads are simply left on the plant.

Welsh Poppies look very pretty in the wild garden and their freshness goes well with ferns. E. A. Bowles had mixed opinions of the plant, but did admit that "a good undertone of yellow meconopsis would look charming under white roses." Provided the roses were a reliably long-lived variety, this display could last for years on end. As Margery Fish challenged: "I defy anyone to control the cheerful and indefatigable Welsh poppy."

The single-flowered, shimmering Poet's Narcissus was, at one point in floriculture, considered the only "true" daffodil. An old, dependable workhorse, *Narcissus poeticus* contributed many of her sparkling characteristics—cold-hardiness, tolerance of dampness, and sweet perfume—to

Pliny said that the name *narcissus* derived from the same root as "narcotic" because of the supposed dizzying effect of the flower's perfume. Some people do get headaches after deeply inhaling narcissus fragrance, which may be connected to the fact that the bulb, which is poisonous if

Narcissus poeticus Amaryllidaceae

POET'S NARCISSUS

PHEASANT'S-EYE NARCISSUS

Poet's Narcissus grows under deciduous shrubs in seaside garden on Long Island, ABOVE. *A mixed bouquet makes a stunning spring display,* OPPOSITE.

the development of other hybrid groups in the genus. Even though flowering late in the spring, when winter dullness already has been swept away by weeks and weeks of colorful spring bulbs, *N. poeticus* still manages to thrill. One writer noted that "the texture of the petals puts them in a separate class, for they have a glittering quality . . . as if each tiny cell was encased with lenses to reflect the light."

William Robinson claimed that Poet's Narcissus was not the narcissus of the Greek poets, but others feel quite strongly that it was. In a Homeric poem describing the kidnapping of Persephone by Pluto, a "silver and purple flower" was created by Zeus as a lure for the unfortunate girl. It seems very poor sportsmanship for two powerful gods to plot against a defenseless girl, but one must not be distracted by this unfair situation and forget the puzzling flower. Buckner Hollingsworth points out that the Greek word for the flower was *narcissus*

and that "Virgil and Pliny, both writing some six or seven hundred years later, describe the narcissus as white and 'purple.'" Apparently, red and purple were somewhat interchangeable in the old days, and thus, Hollingsworth is stubbornly sure that "there is little doubt as to the flower intended. Zeus lured Persephone with a *Narcissus poeticus*." William Robinson is definitely the more famous writer, but, in this case, Hollingsworth's argument seems well substantiated.

ingested, contains lycorine, a drug capable of numbing the nervous system and paralyzing the heart. Perhaps this was the problem with that young Greek, Narcissus, who, fascinated into immobility by his own reflection, eventually died of terminal narcissism.

It must be mentioned that any American gardener with Southern roots who grows anything from the genus *Narcissus* is going to have to decide how to handle dear old Aunt Blanche-Marie from North Carolina. Eighty-one and stubborn as a mule, she will tour the garden, pointing here and there to something that Grandmother Wilson grew, "only much, much bigger." She will finally reach over and, with a look that can only be described as honey over vinegar, ask the only name one dreaded she would. One replies, with all due respect for her eighty-one years of cussedness, and steels oneself for her immediate retort: "Why, those are not narcissus, you fool, those are jonquils."

At this point one has two choices. Quote modern American garden writer Allen Lacy (someone she will respect because he was originally from Texas and not some Yankee barbarian outpost) and tell her that many Southerners use the name "jonquil" inappropriately. Jonquilla Narcissi make up Division Seven (out of eleven divisions) of the genus, so all jonquils are narcissus, but not vice versa. Continuing bravely, one may mention that daffodil is a common name for narcissus, and, ever-prepared, whip out a copy of the Royal Horticultural Society's *Classified List of Daffodil Names* (with 8,000 named cultivated varieties) and a print-out from the Daffodil Data Bank of Des Moines (11,000 varieties). One can even produce *Hortus Third* (in a wheelbarrow, of course) but Aunt Blanche-Marie Wilson Winthrop Smith is going to sniff, walk away, and complain to one's mother how uppity one has become.

Choice two is much more sensible: "Why, Aunt, I do believe you are right! And, as I now recall, Great-Grandmother Wilson grew acres and acres of these same jonquils!" One must swallow all pride and remember that one's own energy is undoubtedly better spent turning the compost pile.

Elizabeth Lawrence wrote authoritatively on bulbs. She mentioned that there were two forms of *Narcissus poeticus* found in old gardens: the large flowered, early blooming *N. p. ornatus*, introduced in 1886; and the smaller, late flowering *N. p.*

The Split-corona Narcissus, ABOVE, *is another old-fashioned favorite delightful in arrangements,* BELOW.

A rainy-day view of a springtime garden, BELOW, *and,* OPPOSITE, *Hales family garden in England.*

recurvus, Old Pheasant's-eye, not recorded in cultivation until the early nineteenth century. It is the latter, intensely scented and with a crimson-fringed crown and central green spot that holds special meaning for flower lovers such as Margery Fish: "Each year I get in a panic that somehow I have lost all my Pheasant-eye narcissi. . . . At last, when one has almost given up hope, its flowers do open, and I think what an idiot I have been to think they would not."

Mrs. Fish liked to plant her Pheasant's-eyes in sunny spots between shrubs. This hides the foliage, which gets "flabby and untidy" after the flower is gone. According to recent Royal Horticultural Society studies at Wisley in Surrey, England, narcissus leaves may be cut eight weeks after the flower has faded, but any earlier will weaken next year's flower. Miss Lawrence planted little purple and white borders of early white iris, Poet's Narcissus, and Sweet Violet. Another charming display can be made by planting Poet's Narcissus among good stands of Maidenhair Fern, both plants sacred to the beleaguered Persephone.

But of course the most extravagant way to enjoy the Poet's Narcissus is to purchase a thousand top-quality bulbs, take the boxes to a favored stretch of grass and open woodland, toss handfuls of bulbs onto the earth, and plant the bulbs as they lie. Generations later, the prodigality will be forgotten, but the gardener's name will be legend.

Nicotiana alata solanaceae

FLOWERING TOBACCO

These two views of Nicotiana demonstrate its night-owl personality. Noontime lethargy and general weariness is apparent, ABOVE LEFT, but as soon as shadows start to lengthen, ABOVE RIGHT, the flowers revive and begin to send forth their perfume.

ico. Nicot took the flower back to Paris, where it was named in his honor and after one of those western hot spots. When *Nicotiana tabacum* was introduced in England, Parkinson wrote about its beauty, sweet scent, and medicinal value. In 1633, Gerard wrote that, according to native custom, leaves of *N. tabacum* were "set on fire, the smoke suckt into the stomach, and thrust forth at the nostrils." Apparently, this barbaric custom is still practiced in some parts of the world.

It wasn't until 1829 that *N. alata,* a tender perennial from Brazil, made its way into the gardens of the world. Some may become disheartened about Nicotiana when they read "tender perennial from Brazil" but there is not one thing difficult about this plant. Treated like an annual, it is no more trouble to grow than petunias, and will reward the gardener's efforts by producing chalky white flowers from June until September.

Deciding where to plant Flowering Tobacco is important. It does not release its perfume during the day, and the plants are covered with soft, sticky hairs that collect dust which is impossible to wash off. It rarely looks its best in bright sunshine, so plan to place this flower in the back of the border or in nice big pots that can be moved about. Nicotiana is wonderful placed near garden seats, under bedroom windows, or any other place where it has a chance to waft luscious perfume into the air—a night owl at its very best.

Almost everyone has at least one friend who is like *Nicotiana alata:* Tired and sulky during daylight hours, Flowering Tobacco perks up as soon as the sun goes down. By moonlight, it is in full glory, arrayed in starry white, and tossing sweet perfume into the darkness. These are the people, and plants, that make staying up late worthwhile.

Another member of the genus *Ni-cotiana* was named as a result of sixteenth century travels that rival the pace of modern jet-setting. While on duty in Portugal, Jean Nicot (1530–1600), an agent of the King of France, met a Dutch merchant who had seeds from a marvelously fragrant flower. He called the flower "tobacco" because the plant had first been introduced either from Tobago. in the West Indies or Tabasco, Mex-

Papaver Papaveraceae

Papaver somniferum
OPIUM POPPY
Papaver rhoeas
FIELD POPPY
Papaver orientale
ORIENTAL POPPY
Papaver nudicaule
ICELAND POPPY

The flamboyant, sun-loving poppy is one of the ancient world's most potent symbols. The genus name derives from Latin, *papa,* thick milk, and refers to the opium made from the juice of the Opium Poppy—certainly the most notorious aspect of this beautiful group of flowers. Gardeners have long been aware that the flower also has equally strong positive qualities. In *The American Flower Garden,* Neltje Blanchan describes the island garden of Celia Thaxter:

Poppies, as she grew them in her garden by the thousand, outlined against the summer sea, were a vision of beauty that no one who saw them can ever forget . . . and Childe Hassam's paintings of the lovely pageant have fortunately preserved the spirit of her sea-girt garden, which was as wild and free as the sea itself.

It is the wild beauty of poppies that makes them so appealing; thankfully, there is a poppy to fit any garden's requirements.

Papaver somniferum is the Opium Poppy, said to have sprung up as a

A border of mixed poppies in a lush Georgia garden, OPPOSITE. *Papaver somniferum* and seedheads, ABOVE.

result of an impetuous act of self-mutilation committed by the Buddha. Desiring to stay awake, Buddha cut off his eyelids. Where they fell, up sprang the mauve petals of the flower. The sleep motif of this gruesome little tale continues uninterrupted throughout history, and as the use of opium has been recognized for so long, it seems quite outside the point of a garden book to recite a dreadful litany of abuse. Gardeners grow *P. somniferum* for much more pleasant reasons, and we may as well leave it at that.

Thomas Jefferson was pleased with the white Opium Poppy he grew in a featured location at Monticello, and the double carnation- and peony-flowered types were known and admired by Gerard. *P. somniferum* is an annual and stands approximately four feet (around one meter) high. Smooth, grayish-blue foliage serves as a perfect foil for the large flowers that are available in almost any color from white to purple. The seed capsules are a striking feature of the plant, looking like little urns perched on long poles. When the wind blows, these containers sway and spill their many seeds, assuring the gardener of a fresh crop of *P. somniferum* each year.

Another annual poppy is *Papaver rhoeas,* the Field, Flanders, or Corn Poppy, which has sown itself so prettily throughout the grain fields of Europe. This delicate-looking flower is bright crimson. Its petals are a good source of red pigment, suitable for use in wines and medi-

P. rhoeas, *the Field Poppy,* ABOVE, *is the parent of the spectacular Shirley Poppies,* OPPOSITE.

P. nudicaule, *the Iceland Poppy,* ABOVE, *is a perennial from the far north. The showy* P. orientale, *or Oriental Poppy,* BELOW.

cines. While the Field Poppy is by no means as potent as *P. somniferum,* it does have narcotic qualities that were recognized as early as Culpeper's time. Jefferson grew this poppy as well and naturalized it in the Grove at Monticello. It is, of course, famous as the Flanders Poppy of World War I. *P. rhoeas* is also famous as a parent, for its children, the nothing-short-of-fabulous Shirley Poppies, are some of the most pleasing flowers to have come into cultivation within the last century.

Shirley does not refer to a woman, but, instead to the vicarage in England where, in the summer of 1880, the Reverend Wilks noticed that one of the wild poppies in his garden had a tiny, but striking, band of white around the margins of its petals. He marked the flower, saved the seed, and began to select and develop a definite type of poppy that would retain the airy grace of its wild parent, but would sport silky, sherbet-colored petals with a vanilla-ice edge. The flower became an instant success, and between developing the Shirleys and serving as Secretary of the Royal Horticultural Society for thirty-two years, one wonders when the industrious Reverend Wilks ever found time to write a sermon.

Two other poppies, *P. orientale* and *P. nudicaule,* echo the form and colors of *P. somniferum* and *P. rhoeas,* yet have the added benefit of being perennials.

The Oriental Poppy was discovered by Tournefort in 1702 and was

proudly brought back to France for the enjoyment of Louis XIV. Its popularity was instant and, by 1741, Peter Collinson, the London Quaker who was part of the trans-Atlantic network of Quaker plant and flower admirers, had seeds in England to send to his colleague in Philadelphia, John Bartram.

The success of *P. orientale* is no secret to anyone who has seen this most showy of poppies, considered by some as among the noblest of hardy plants. It makes large clumps of thistle-like foliage setting off huge red or pink flowers with shiny black centers. It is the foliage of the plant that presents the only hitch to the gardener: Just when one has enjoyed the flowers about as much as any flower can be enjoyed, *P. orientale* goes into a dormant funk that can leave an awesome gap in the border.

Gertrude Jekyll, who designed more than two hundred gardens, had a famous gap remedy. Her cure was to have clouds of Baby's Breath (*Gypsophila paniculata*) ready to billow over the hole like vapor over a volcano crater. Others use *Thalictrum aquilegifolium*. Whatever succession plant is chosen, it must be something wonderful enough to help the gardener forget the only shortcoming of an otherwise outstanding flower. Try not to think of the hole, but instead recall E. A. Bowles's be-

The large colorful Oriental Poppy needs room to show off. Due to its disappearing act, it also requires a successor.

loved pink Oriental Poppy, which he said looked "like a strawberry ice on a frosted glass plate."

Ice brings to mind the last member of the genus to be discussed here, *Papaver nudicaule,* Iceland Poppy. This is similar in form to the Corn Poppy, delicate and smaller than the *P. somniferum* or *P. orientale. Papaver nudicaule* came into cultivation in 1730 from the far northern regions of Canada and Siberia. It is pleasant to imagine the delight of the explorers who discovered these yellow flowers gloriously thriving in golden subarctic meadows bathed in neverending summer light. Today the flower is available in many colors, and although it is called a perennial, should be treated like a biennial.

The Iceland Poppy makes lovely flower arrangements if care is taken in gathering the flower. Just before the bud is ready to open, it will stand up straight; this is the time to cut the flower, preferably in the cool of the evening or early morning. Quickly dip the end of each stem in boiling water and then plunge the flower up to its neck in cold water and let it rest. Soon the buds will open and the flowers will last for days in arrangements that appear as ethereal as butterfly wings.

Perhaps Robert Burns did not know the boiling water trick when he wrote *Tam O'Shanter,* but his lines stand as one of loveliest poetic references to the genus: "But pleasures are like poppies spread/ You seize the flower, its bloom is shed."

Phlomis samia Labiatae

Phlomis is one of the few plants described in *Hortus Third* that actually looks as strange as it sounds: "lvs. ovate-cordate, tomentose, long-petioled; verticillasters 12-20 fld; bractlets subulate, glandular tomentose; calyx teeth subulate." In plain English, Phlomis is a strangely handsome plant with flowers borne in circles around the stem, tier upon tier, like little space ships flying one on top of the other. Although Phlomis is easy to grow, there are not many species in cultivation. But, once you observe and enjoy its sculptural quality, Phlomis is a difficult plant to resist.

Very little has been written about this plant and, perhaps the most unusual aspect of *Phlomis samia* is that it seems to have not one single folk name. Even derivation of the genus name is somewhat obscure. Some books say that Phlomis is the old Greek name for Dioscorides (c. A.D. 40–90), author of *De Materia Medica* about medicinal plants. Others insist that it is from *phlomos,* the down used to make wicks. In 1759, Philip Miller wrote that Phlomis leaves were good medicine for sore throats, but other than this information, this plant seems to be a mystery.

There are shrubby phlomises, the most well-known being *Phlomis fruticosa* or Jerusalem Sage. Another herbaceous species is called *Phlomis russelliana,* but *P. samia,* discovered in the mountains of North Africa in 1714, is the oldest type in cultivation. It grows three to four feet (around 1 m) tall, has creamy yellow flowers in May and June, and in the southern United States, has evergreen leaves. *P. samia* is easily grown in ordinary soil, is blissfully free of pests and diseases, and will generally take care of itself in the wild garden or in open positions in wide borders.

Phlomis samia is the perfect plant for gardeners who suffer from know-it-all guests. Its handsome carriage and weirdly wonderful flowers make it impossible to ignore, but even the most irritatingly well-informed visitor will likely have to beg for the name. Then the proud gardener may enjoy that supreme moment when he can coolly identify an unusual plant and quote a well respected gardener (in this case, William Robinson): Oh? That beautiful plant? Surely you know *Phlomis samia*—"interesting because it is so unlike most other plants."

Phlomis is a statuesque member of the Mint Family that grows three to four feet tall. It has no special requirements and remains evergreen in mild climates.

Polemonium

JACOB'S LADDER

Every child who ever went to summer camp has suffered through hours of verses belonging to that old dirge, "We Are Climbing Jacob's Ladder." Little ones everywhere must wonder "Where does one go when one gets to the top of Jacob's old ladder, anyway?" Surely the answer is meant to be heaven, but this sad song makes one wonder.

These musings are strictly beside the point, except that *Polemonium caeruleum* is also called Jacob's Ladder and is happy in as many ways as the song is not. This hardy perennial makes airy tufts of foliage that look like hundreds of little green ladders, all piled on top of each other. One might imagine tiny creatures climbing up and swinging upon a graceful, swaying raceme of blue flowers.

Caeruleum means dark blue, but medium blue better describes these flowers. The plant has been in cultivation since Roman times, but is probably not the exact one that Pliny wrote about. *Polemos* means war, and there was indeed a war fought between two princes over who discovered Pliny's plant. Pliny's description, however, of a plant "with thick clusters of berries," just does not sound like Jacob's Ladder. Unfortunately, scientific fact often ruins romantic stories.

Polemonium caeruleum is considered indigenous to the northern parts of Great Britain. In *A Handbook to British Flora,* published at the turn of the century, the author argues that it has been in cottage gardens for so many centuries, and sows itself so successfully, that perhaps it is a naturalized rather than an indigenous species. This splitting of hairs should alert the gardener that Jacob's Ladder is one of the easiest plants to grow. It likes deep, well-drained, rich loam, and sun. And those in northern climates who are fed up with winter-kill in the garden may take heart: *P. caeruleum* is abundant in the meadows of Lapland.

For those who cannot leave well enough alone, there is a white form of Jacob's Ladder, plus another variety with variegated leaves (which might better be called Painter's Ladder). But for those satisfied with what is already beautiful, take the advice of Alice Morse Earle and grow the blue form—"an old-fashioned plant, but well worth universal cultivation."

This old-fashioned blue flower has been in gardens since the days of the Roman Empire. A garden bench amid a profusion of Polemonium in an English garden, OPPOSITE.

caeruleum Polemoniaceae

There is nothing new about calling February horrible names, but it is late March that more often becomes the last straw for the winter-weary. For those surviving in what is termed "the northeast corridor" of America, the end of the first quarter means wading oceans of half-frozen water and navigating mountains of soot-blackened ice. During this trying period, even the most promising commodities broker or the most sensible corporate lawyer may succumb to what used to be called "the vapors."

"A nice little get-away" is the modern cure for this old-fashioned malady, and Caribbean air fares soar during March. A less obvious cure is an early spring trip to Devon, England, where the soft climate can soothe uneasy spirits. In that slice of heaven one can unwind among green, rolling hills, and relax into the coziness of an unspoiled country inn. After several days of being nourished with gravy-filled meat pies and fruit tarts with clotted cream, one regains strength and a desire to venture away from the fire and Jane Austen to explore the countryside. It is then that the most effective part of the Devon Cure will take place. From late March to May the West Country landscape is carpeted in Primroses. They grow everywhere—in gardens, in woods, along hedgerows, even along the railway lines. And no one, not even the most nervous, can ignore their simple beauty. The mere act of gazing upon a wooded bank with pale yellow, sweetly scented Primroses will take knots from the neck, twitches from the limbs, and will undoubtedly give the discoverer his or her best night's sleep since leaving the crib. Simply put, to find Primroses is to find peace.

If this all seems impossibly romantic, there is historic documentation of the mood-elevating power of Primroses. The venerable figures involved are no less than Benjamin Disraeli (Earl of Beaconsfield) and

Monticello, naturalized under hedges and in shady walks, their sweet scent and delicate blossoms ready to cure writer's block for the author of the Declaration of Independence.

Stick with simple Primroses for simple pleasures. All one needs to grow them is a spot reminiscent of Devon: moist, shady, and cool. Failure with this flower is usually due to excess heat or drought, so be sure to place them in the woods, in the shady border, or under deciduous

Primula vulgaris Primulaceae

Queen Victoria. Disraeli became Queen Victoria's Prime Minister in 1868, seven years after the death of her beloved Prince, Albert. This distinguished statesman was worldly, dapper, devoted to his Queen, and eventually became close enough to her to confide that Primroses were his favorite flowers. This personal touch seemed to delight the sad widow and, shortly after, the exchange of Primroses became a ritual between them. This delightful custom continued until 1881, when Disraeli died. The importance of this intimate exchange was such that Disraeli's followers eventually formed "The Primrose League" in honor of the departed flower-fancying Conservative statesman.

Primula comes from *primus,* meaning the first, and not only is the Primrose one of the very first

ENGLISH PRIMROSE

The Hales family of Devon, England, created a pretty Primrose path, OPPOSITE. *A Devonshire hedgerow,* ABOVE.

flowers of spring, but it was also one of the very first flowers, along with daisies and violas, to be carried inside medieval castle walls. They probably came in with turf meant for building rudimentary seats, but soon became a popular element in the domestic scene. Primrose pudding was a favorite Elizabethan dessert, and although New England settlers probably found the other ingredients (almond milk and powdered ginger among them) difficult to come by, Primroses were grown in the early ornamental gardens at Williamsburg. By 1771, Primroses were growing at

shrubs. (Evergreens are even better.) Primroses can take a good deal of nasty weather, so plant them in the autumn, cover lightly with leaves for winter, and begin making furtive peeks underneath as early as March, if the weather is friendly. One point agreed on by all Primrose buffs is the need to divide the plants. Every year, or at least every other year, the plants should be lifted, split and the resulting single rosettes replanted in the shade. The best time to do this is during the first damp spell after flowering.

A garden writer once wrote that "England displays a rose on the royal coat of arms, but she carries a primrose in her heart." To this one can only add that a Primrose in the heart has just got to be the most charming antidote there is for a dreary day.

LUNGWORT
SOLDIERS AND
SAILORS *Pulmonaria officinalis*

Lungwort is an early-blooming, hardy perennial with beautiful leaves spotted with green and white. In early spring, while the leaves are still inconspicuous, small, rosy, tube-shaped flowers appear. As individual flowers mature, they change from pink to purple, and, finally, to rich shades of blue, with the happy result that all three colors often appear on the same stem.

Most people like the calico effect of Lungwort's flowers, but there is not one hundred percent agreement concerning the leaves. Alice Morse Earle said that "all spotted leaves . . . which show the slightest resemblance to the markings of a snake or lizard, always fill me with dislike." Sigmund Freud would have been most interested in Morse's comments, but most people find Pulmonaria's bold foliage to be its outstanding feature.

Lungwort's leaves figured prominently in the early sixteenth century Doctrine of Signatures, according to which the plant's spots looked like lung spots and thus both the common and botanical names were born. This reference is, of course, another less than savory allusion to the leaves, but they are actually lovely and cheery on a dull day.

One old book called this plant Jesus-Joseph-and-Mary, but this might get confused with profanity if said with too much enthusiasm. It is also called Lady's Tears for Mary's sufferings and where it's known by this name, it is considered very unlucky to uproot or otherwise disturb the plant. Soldier-and-his-Wife, Soldiers and Sailors and Boys-and-Girls are names referring to the pink and blue flowers. One particularly appealing name is Spotted Dog.

Other species in the genus are *Pulmonaria angustifolia* and *Pulmonaria saccharata*. The latter has gone overboard with leaf spots that have widened into splots, and the former has no spots at all. A form of *Pulmonaria officinalis* has only white flowers, but all three of these seem to completely miss the point of Pulmonaria. Keep the distinct spots, keep the multi-colored flowers, and stick to the best-known species of the genus.

Pulmonaria pops up early in spring, flowers, and then makes dense tufts of foliage. As the leaves enlarge and elongate, the plant creates a good ground cover, perfect in a wild or woodland garden. It can also be used in borders and will brighten the bare earth of spring. This plant does best in partially shaded, moist soil. Grown as a salute to old cottage gardens, Pulmonaria's heart-shaped leaves, which Margery Fish described "as rough as a calf's tongue," will delight viewers for months.

P. officinalis, LEFT, *has distinct spots and pink and blue flowers similar to those of* P. saccharata, RIGHT. *Lungwort makes good ground cover.*

Boraginaceae

RUGOSA ROSE *Rosa rugosa* Rosaceae

Evidence in Colorado Oligocene deposits shows that roses grew there at least 35 million years ago, making it clear that the subject of antique roses is, indeed, formidable.

The poet merrily writes: "Oh! No man knows/ Through what wild centuries/ Roves the Rose," but garden writers just can't take it that easy. Even some Grand Old Rosarians—Graham Stuart Thomas, Sacheverell Sitwell, and Edward Bunyard—were clearly awed by the topic of their respective outstanding books. Like a humble knight, Thomas dedicated *Old Shrub Roses* (1956) "to all those who have helped in the Quest." He described pilgrimages to various old rose gardens left intact after World War II, including one to Sacheverell Sitwell's "splendid collection" at Weston Hall in England. Sitwell had earlier published a short chapter in *Old Fashioned Flowers* (1939) that begins: "This chapter on Old fashioned Roses is written in humility and diffidence. . . . It would be quite impossible for an amateur with but a few years' experience to dispute the studies of a lifetime." Sitwell then cites Bunyard's *Old Garden Roses* (1937) as "a book so full of knowledge that it is a presumption to touch upon his subject." But even Bunyard, considered by most as the apex of this rosarian triumvirate, felt the weightiness of his topic: "It might almost be said that the Rose is an index of civilization." Yet it is entirely possible for mere mortals to grow and enjoy old roses.

Serious rose growers refer to serious books for information on the thousands of wild and man-made roses. Historic itineraries and family trees for the Gallica Rose, the Bourbon Rose, and hosts of others are readily available, but there's also a lot of inessential rose information that's fun to know.

Roses are native as far north as the Arctic Circle *(Rosa acicularis),* but no rose has ever been found growing wild in the southern hemisphere. The first work of art with a rose *(Rosa sancta)* was found by Sir Arthur Evans in a fresco in Crete and is dated 2000 B.C. Confucius (551–478 B.C.) documented early rose culture by the Chinese, and Theophrastus (372–287 B.C.) wrote about use of the flower by the ancient Greeks. The Romans were crazy about roses, spread them all over Europe, and generally used them in such decadent ways that early Christian leaders refused to allow the flower in churches. Memories of debaucheries faded, however, and the rosary was invented. Rosaries were originally

This huge hedge of Rosa rugosa *acts as protection for a seaside garden against salty ocean winds,* OPPOSITE. *Rugosa in September,* ABOVE.

composed of beads made from compressed rose petals, in memory of the rose wreath given to St. Dominick by the Virgin Mary. The oldest known rosebush *(Rosa canina)* is at Hildesheim Cathedral in Germany and is claimed to be 1000 years old.

Rose hips have as much as twenty times the vitamin C of orange juice. Everyone can imagine rose jam and rose pudding, but an equally popular Elizabethan dish was rose petals and calf's brains. Another odd taste combination was created when rose petals were used as scented filters for cigarettes.

The first rose breeding in North America took place in Charleston, South Carolina, in the garden of John Champneys, in the early 1800s. By 1900, there were several thousand named roses, and today's count soars above 12,000.

Which old rose to grow? Edward Bunyard wrote that he did not know of any more richly scented rose than *Rosa rugosa* 'Parfum de l'Hay': "a contralto scent in contrast with the Tea's soprano." Graham Stuart Thomas wrote that *R. rugosa* and *R. moschata* (Musk Rose) "are the species, which in my experience, float their fragrance on the air with the greatest abandon, sometimes more than 100 yards." Thomas also later wrote that the China Rose and *R. rugosa* are almost alone among the old roses in producing flowers from May to October.

Rose expert Roy Genders recommends Rugosas because of their exceptional winter-hardiness (they are

Old Blush, ABOVE, *was introduced in the mid-eighteenth century. Madame Isaac Pereire,* RIGHT, *dated 1881, thrives in a day lily collection.*

used as understocks for tender roses), their tolerance of salt spray and poor soil, and their resistance to black spot and mildew. Another rose expert, Malcomb Lowe, also loves Rugosas because they are drought-resistant, tolerate "wet feet," require no pruning, and many of them will survive temperatures as low as −35°F.

Allen Lacy gets right to the point of rose choices by quoting a list of "What Can Go Wrong With Roses": mottling, mildew, blasted buds, distorted flowers, Japanese beetles, and off-color leaves. He does not grow some roses for all those reasons. But, he adds, "I do grow rugosas."

With all their sterling qualities, it is a wonder more Rugosas are not grown. They certainly qualify as antique. Edward Bunyard believed that a white Rugosa was grown in

Chinese gardens from a very early date and, in his book, he reproduces a drawing by Chao Ch'ang (active A.D. 1000) that has a very pretty Rugosa in it. The first Rugosas were brought to Europe from Japan and China in 1784 and were introduced in Britain by a London nurseryman named Lee. They obviously caught on fast because McMahon's basic list of "Hardy and Deciduous Trees and Shrubs," published in 1806 in the newly independent America, offered "*Rosa rugosa,* the wrinkled leave rose." It is odd that everyone seems to list all the other old roses first— Gallicas, Bourbons, Chinas—and leaves the hardy, disease-resistant, fragrant, pretty Rugosa until the end.

The Rugosas certainly look primitively beautiful. They are densely prickled and big as a healthy country bumpkin. Their leaves are ruggedly wrinkled instead of smooth, and turn lovely colors in autumn. The shrub can grow to six feet (2 m) and will flower, more or less continuously, from May until October, displaying magenta, rose, or white blossoms, either single or semi-double. The flowers have a robust clove scent that wafts throughout the garden. As the flowers go over, large red hips begin to form, and as the season progresses, flowers and hips appear on the same shrub in a most decorative manner. These roses look and are almost indestructible.

Even the most casually equipped gardener can plant and care for Rugosas. The only essential item is a pair of Serious, Thick Gloves—

cheap garden gloves will soon have one swearing from prickle pain. In addition one needs a Digging Implement, and Something That Cuts.

Malcomb Lowe, a rose grower in New Hampshire, says to plant Rugosas in the autumn. "A spring-planted bush does not have time to develop a sound root system before leafing out, and is thus more susceptible to disease, insects, and fungus."

As for the dreaded pruning, Rugosas have a wonderful trait that renders this chore quite simple. They bloom on both old and new wood, so there is absolutely no need to prune at all unless to remove old bark-bound canes. However, if one does want to shape the shrub or control its size, Rugosas will tolerate very hard clipping. Some nurserymen recommend cutting them back to five inches (12 cm) over the winter (before the sap starts) to ensure a proliferation of canes and blooms. But pruning is a matter of preference: Rugosas that have never felt the touch of steel bloom just fine.

Propagation is no problem with Rugosas. Stem cuttings can be stuck directly into the ground and covered with upended gallon jars, forming mini-greenhouses for moisture and protection. Or the ends can be first stuck into a magic potion discovered by Dr. Makota Kawase in Ohio and

Other antiques include pink Seven Sisters and Harison's Yellow at Whipple House in Massachusetts.

endorsed by those wild Rose Rustlers of Texas. Soak one-inch lengths of freshly cut willow shoots in a small amount of water overnight. This releases rhizocaline, a substance that promotes root growth, into the water. Soak the ends of the rose cuttings in the willow water for twenty-four hours, and then stick them in the earth as described.

Perhaps the most classic use of Rugosa is as a hedge—so beautiful and fragrant as to please the grumpiest neighbor and so tough that it's used as a crash barrier between highway lanes. Yet the sprays of buds can be used as cut flowers, with petals dropping after twenty-four hours, but flowers opening each day.

For all those who don't plant roses because they seem so complicated, think Rugosa. If you have a small garden, plant a specimen and keep it clipped. If you enjoy a large space, go for Browning's "roses, roses, all the way," but please pick another less sentimental poet to quote when guests are swept away by the magnificent display. Edward Lear (1812–1888) suits the happy Rugosa just fine:

And this is certain; if so be
You could just now my garden see
The aspic of my flowers so bright
Would make you shudder with delight.

And if you voz to see my roziz
As is a boon to all men's noziz—
You'd fall upon your back and scream—
"O Lawk! O cricky! It's a dream!"

CLARY *Salvia sclarea* Labiatae

There are many beautiful sages. Unfortunately, there is also one, *Salvia splendens,* which is inexplicably popular since it belongs only in the Ugly Garden. When the genus offers almost every shade of blue, mauve, purple, rose, and white flowers, why must "the silent scream of scarlet sage" be endured? Why not instead have a plant that smells lovely, is statuesque, has softly colored flowers, and can even be eaten? Clary fills all the above requirements with such willingness that one can only hope the dear old thing has never met its shocking Brazilian relative.

Clary is native to the Mediterranean area and, along with Rosemary, Lavender, Balm, and Thyme, "grew up" along with the ancient civilizations based there. When sizable armies left this area, to tame barbarians and to conduct other business, Clary and the rest went along. In England, they later became standard material in monastery gardens and eventually went to private gardens, grand and humble alike. Today Clary is still grown for home winemaking, is used in fine perfumery, and is essential in the muscatel and vermouth formulas.

Even if one is inclined to leave brewing and distilling to the experts, Clary has many culinary uses. The large, heart-shaped leaves appear early in the season and can be used—fresh, dried, or frozen—for both savory and sweet dishes.

John Parkinson, author of *Paradisi in Sole Paradisus Terrestris,* grew Clary in his kitchen garden and no

Dusky purple Clary flourishes in the strong sun of a seaside garden, OPPOSITE *and* ABOVE.

doubt partook of it in some form or another. One early use was in a popular dish that consisted of whole leaves, dipped in a batter of egg yolks, flour, and milk, and fried in butter. These crispy bits were served as a side dish with meat and, today can still make an innovative alternative to *pommes frites.* An elegant recipe for a Clary dessert was favored by John Evelyn, the influential seventeenth-century dilettante and garden designer, who ate dainty omelettes of Clary leaves, cream, and eggs, cooked in butter and seasoned with sugar and lemon.

Clary is actually a biennial or perennial, but is usually treated as an annual, raised each year from seeds or from nursery stock. The large, slightly hairy leaves appear early (this is the best time to eat them) and, around July, tall spires of pale rosy-lavender flowers will begin. The plants are large, three feet (1 m) tall and about as wide, so think in shrub sizes when deciding where to plant them. Clary looks pretty in the

kitchen garden, fits nicely in the border, and may naturalize itself in the wild garden. It will make masterful forms on a sunny, dry bank where the pale flowers turn ghostly during twilight.

Although Clary is very popular in New England and in England, this is one cottage plant that won't let the southern gardener down. Whereas some old plants, like primulas and some dianthus, will just frizzle and die if exposed to too much heat and sun, salvias only attain their full glory, and their distinct muscatel scent, when the weather is hot and dry. When all else is limply wilted or fried crispy, this Mediterranean native stands tall like the gladiator of the garden.

Clary has many characteristics to recommend it, but the whole truth is, that with the exception of the "silent screamer," there are lots of other salvias that are equally wonderful. For those who find themselves increasingly attracted to the genus, there is a mecca for devotees. Chelsea Physic Garden in London, established in 1673 and ever young and dynamic, is—among many other things—the center for research on *Salvia* taxonomy. There, along the banks of the Thames, one can wander past beautiful beds with salvias of every size, shape, smell, and shade, and participate in a tradition of study and observation that spans three centuries. Chelsea Physic Garden is a wonderful treat for all who sow, weed, mulch, and dream in their gardens.

LONDON PRIDE · *Saxifraga umbrosa*

London Pride causes great speculation among those who theorize upon how Earth looked millions of years ago. *Saxifraga umbrosa* grows abundantly in the mountains around Killarney, Ireland, and also appears prolifically in Portugal, western Spain, and the Pyrenees. Because London Pride shares these exact same habitats with *Arbutus unedo* (Strawberry Tree) and several types of insects, many scientists believe that these

two areas, now hundreds of miles apart, were once connected to a common mainland. This information has little to do with gardening, but it is quite fun to imagine Ireland under the gray clouds of the Atlantic—festooned with pink drifts of London Pride and Strawberry Trees and inhabited by some little buzzing insects—dreamily floating away from primordial Europe upon a magical, foggy ocean current.

Although the name Saxifrage comes from *saxum* (rock) and *frangere* (to break), there is no way that London Pride is deemed responsible for the breaking away of the Emerald Isle. The name instead refers to the plant's traditional use in medicine: "There are not many better medicines to break the [kidney] stone than this," reported an enthusiastic Culpeper. The specific epithet *umbrosa* means shady and London Pride is

where few other things will live." Oddly enough, these are the exact words that William Robinson used to describe the plant in his book, so if one has some cold shade, there seems to be total agreement from both sides of the Atlantic that London Pride is the perfect plant to go there. It does have an excellent reputation for flowering without complaint, and its only foible is that it quickly dies in very hot climates.

There is nothing like London Pride to brighten and lighten those heavy, damp corners that lurk in every town or country garden. The spreading leaves are evergreen in mild climates and can make dense tufts about four inches high and about one foot in diameter (10 cm × 30 cm). These may become tinged with crimson in winter; London Pride always looks pretty, even when not in flower.

The flowers are lovely, though. Sometime in early summer, wiry, erect stems start to grow and produce loose, fluffy panicles of tiny pale pink flowers. These are ever so slightly dotted with red, as if splatter-painted by a kindergarten class of fairy babies. If planted in cool locations, *S. umbrosa* will naturalize, creating quite a magical effect in lowland woods in May.

Saxifragaceae

in a section of the genus requiring shady locations.

The common name London Pride arose from this hardy little perennial's ability to survive the pollution-ridden atmosphere of nineteenth-century London, and although a city-slicker, it was also popular in provincial cottage gardens. In 1917 Robert McCurdy wrote that "Nancy-Pretty [another folk name] has always been a favorite in English cottage gardens,

but never used in America to great extent." Another flower called "London Pride " was popular in nineteenth-century American dooryard gardens, but this was actually *Lychnis coronaria,* more commonly called Rose Campion.

One old American garden book lists *S. umbrosa* in a compilation of "Best Survivors of Old-Fashioned Garden Flowers," and says that "it will thrive in the cold shade of walls

sedum telephium Crassulaceae

ORPINE
LIVE-FOREVER

Orpine has been in English gardens and folklore for so many centuries that its date of introduction is unknown. Sedum spectabile, RIGHT, has a stiff carriage and ungraceful flower.

In *Early American Gardens: For Meate or Medicine* the delightful Ann Leighton wrote about this plant as if it were a beloved pet. "Orpine seems to be one of those plants which follows and stays with man. . . . Called

Live-Forever, it shares with those plants called Everlasting a domestic decoration niche." With no culinary purposes and insignificant curative powers, Orpine was the lapdog of early American gardens—faithful and pretty, but of no practical use.

Now that gardeners no longer have to feed and cure their families from a plot outside the door, Orpine's beauty alone makes it a useful plant, especially since its rosy-purple prime comes during that awkward Indian summer period when yellows and golds seem to heat the garden with leaping flames.

Sedum telephium is one of very few sedums native to Great Britain, but as an old *Handbook of British Flora* admits, "it has been so long cultivated in cottage gardens, and is so very tenacious of life, that it is very difficult to say how far it is really indigenous." Tenacity of life made Orpine's decorative qualities even more endearing to cottagers. In olden days, they would cut Orpine from the garden on Midsummer's Day, hang it from the ceiling, and there it would remain green until Christmas Day. This became an early good-luck charm and source of the folk-name Midsummer-Men.

Orpine comes from a large, well-known genus named from the Latin "to sit" *(sedere),* and over 600 species of sedum may be found perching on walls, rocks, or roofs across the north temperate zone. *Sedum spectabile* is an old, reliable plant that, according to naturalist Miriam Rothschild, "exerts a magical attraction for the small Tortoiseshell Butterfly." Unfortunately, *S. spectabile* also bears a comical resemblance to broccoli. *Sedum roseum* is cultivated mainly for its rose-scented roots, useful in potpourri. Two other species have intriguing names: *Sedum sexangulare,* or Love-Entangled; and *S. acre,* the famous Welcome-Home-Husband-Be-Ye-Ever-So-Drunk.

Orpine is one of the most variable stonecrops and, by the turn of the century, more than twenty forms had received names as subspecies or varieties. Robinson claimed that the common native plant was "as showy as any of these," and it is only in recent times that this venerable perennial became scarce in gardens. Gertrude Jekyll's selected clone 'Munstead Red' has overshadowed the species for some years, but its dark, brownish-red flower actually seems a bit muddy next to the clear rosy purple of the original.

Orpine has pale green stems with an erect, tufting habit, although sometimes the stems may flop a bit. The leaves are oval, slightly scalloped, and a pretty gray-green. Little dabs of purple flowers may appear nestled with the leaves along the stem. The terminal flower heads are only two to four inches across (5 cm × 10 cm), making Orpine a decidedly daintier plant than broccoli-like *S. spectabile.* Shade-tolerance is another distinction of the plant, and, coupled with its incredible drought-resistance, Orpine proves itself useful indeed.

Orpine was very popular in eighteenth-century borders, and it is also nice underplanting autumn blooming roses or alongside white colchicums. Sedums and September go together, and Orpine is the real poppet of the genus.

There are various theories about teaching a child to enjoy the garden. A very silly one requires that the little one be led into the vegetable patch to sow a row of quick-growing radishes. Yes, harvest time will soon arrive, but what four-year-old loves to eat radishes? Another theoretical child-pleaser is the towering, nodding sunflower—an insult to a child's love of subtlety and, perhaps, even monstrous to the easily frightened.

The best way to interest a little boy or girl in gardening involves two principles. The first: never force a child to work in the garden. A reluctant weeder or raker may, later in life, take the dreaded road to low- or no-maintenance gardening. Even one afternoon's worth of begrudged assistance could lead to a lifetime of plastic flowers and Astroturf. The second principle: a child must be allowed to pick flowers. This is a tough one and requires great courage on the part of the grown-up gardener; however, given a very small vase and a pair of training scissors, most children will rise to the occasion and create a beautifully innocent arrangement that not only leaves the borders intact but also delivers enough charm to make up for the crayon marks in the hallway. Some plants to grow for child-picking are Sweet Alyssum for smell, Mint for taste, and Lamb's Ears for feel.

Stachys byzantina Labiatae

LAMB'S EARS

Lamb's Ears growing in Somerset, England, A B O V E. *The velvety foliage makes excellent ground cover and is favored by children.*

Stachys byzantina is absolutely enmeshed in confusion over its botanical name. It was long known as *S. lanata,* Graham Stuart Thomas calls it *S. olympica,* and *Hortus* calls it *byzantina.* That is the name used here. Lamb's Ears avoids confusion and most people seem to recognize this common name.

Lamb's Ears entered cultivation in England in 1782 from the Caucasus and became a well-loved cottage favorite. Mrs. Earle, author of *Potpourri from a Surrey Garden* (1897), wrote that "not the smallest or driest garden should be without this plant," but obviously its popularity suffered an eclipse because it was at one time unavailable from many nurseries. Margery Fish helped rectify this situation by collecting it from cottage gardens, where it was often called Jesus Flannel, and taking it to a nursery for propagation and distribution.

Stachys byzantina was known as Woolly Woundwort in nineteenth-century America, and, despite its reputed dislike for the cold, seems to have managed to survive without too awful a reputation for winterkill. It should be planted in full sun and enjoys ordinary soil. The soft ears will make a lovely mat of silvery velvet and, in June or July, fuzzy spikes will rise about two feet (60 cm) to show off tiny pinkish or mauve flowers. Some people do not like the flowers and cut down the spikes, but these are probably the same people who force children to rake the lawn in the heat of August.

Stachys byzantina makes an excellent ground cover and looks very pretty underneath old roses. In mild climates it is evergreen and will make mats three feet (1 m) across. The stems put down roots as they spread and will fall over a wall gracefully. In climates where it doesn't survive the winter, treat it as an annual and bed out each spring. Even if one has to replant Lamb's Ears every year, it is well worth the bother. Keep in mind that this plant received one of the best plant recommendations ever printed: "Beloved by children, despised by experts."

Tagetes erecta
AFRICAN MARIGOLD

Tagetes patula
FRENCH MARIGOLD

Marigold is a name used almost as often in naming plants as Mary is in naming humans. Mary's Gold was applied to several yellow-flowering plants that bloom in time for festivities honoring the Virgin. There is a Cape Marigold *(Dimorphotheca),* a Fig Marigold *(Mesembryanthemum),* Marsh Marigold *(Caltha),* and Pot Marigold *(Calendula)* and, as with Mary, the name marigold is probably used so often because it is so pretty.

The genus *Tagetes* is entirely New World in origin and can be found from New Mexico to Argentina. Both African and French Marigolds are actually from Mexico and were probably grown in pre-Conquest gardens. Later, seeds were sent back to Spain, and from there, traveled to monastery gardens in North Africa and France. The French Marigold was brought by Huguenot refugees to England in 1573, and the African was "discovered" in a naturalized state in North Africa in 1596. By the time these plants reached a state of

At Monticello, the species form of French Marigold (T. patula) *twines up into plantings of Larkspur.*

general cultivation, their origins were obscure, and the English dubbed them African and French to differentiate them from their own native Pot Marigold, *Calendula officinalis.*

French and African Marigolds were always found in old-fashioned gardens where they were lauded for being easy to cultivate and of a bright disposition, though they were mourned by some for being "useless in hand bouquets." J. W. Gent wrote in 1683 that the African Marigold was a "biggie" flower with a "very Naughty smell." Perhaps scents, like other things, go in and

out of favor because few today find marigold aroma objectionable.

Gerard wrote about *Tagetes erecta* in the *Historie of Plants.* According to his accounts, one should avoid eating both the French or African species. He noted "a boy whose lipps and mouth when he began to chew the floures of *Tagetes erecta* did swell extreamly. Likewise we gave to a cat the floures tempered with fresh cheese and she forthwith mightily swelled and a little while after she died." Pot Marigold *(Calendula)* is fine to eat, and earlier we gave the first lines of a recipe for "Marigold

Tagetes Compositae

Cheese" made with Calendula petals. Care should be taken not to confuse the two genera, as a mistake like this could ruin a garden picnic faster than a hailstorm.

Tagetes patula is the smaller species of the two included here. Moderate in height as well as size of flower, *T. patula* has yellow or orange flowers, either single or double, with crinkled, velvety petals (which are really ray florets). Sometimes these petals or florets are marked with red or brown. It usually grows about one to two feet (30 to 60 cm) tall. The French Marigold was especially popular with eighteenth-century florists and created quite a rage at exhibitions, so the prejudice against Marigold scent was obviously on the wane by that time.

Tagetes patula is revered by organic gardeners for being a natural deterrent to garden pests, and it is especially helpful in the kitchen garden. A combination of Sweet Alyssum and French Marigold makes a beautiful lacy edging for a row of loose-leaf lettuce, and, with a few tomato plants added along the back, one has the beginnings of a pretty and pest-free salad garden. (Do *not* eat the Marigolds. See above.)

French Marigolds are also pretty growing next to blue flowers. At Monticello they are allowed to reach up through plantings of Larkspur and to billow onto the path. It is not difficult to use *T. patula* in ways more creative than bedding-out, especially since the species form has a pleasing, almost vine-like appearance.

Also at Monticello, the single-flowered species form of the brightly colored African Marigold (T. erecta), ABOVE.

Marigolds have been popular for centuries and have been bred in various shapes and colors.

Tagetes erecta is larger than *T. patula* in every way. African Marigolds have clear yellow or orange flowers, two to three inches (3 cm) in diameter, and grow about three feet high (1 m). Eighteenth-century gardeners bragged about growing them as tall as five feet (1.5 m).

Gerard grew this plant in his garden, and Thomas Jefferson grew it at Monticello, but some gardeners today find the large, bright plants of African Marigolds "just a little too much." This is a shame, because there are very few truly ugly flowers, but instead, flowers that are simply not used well. Those who have hitherto concealed a fondness for the big-hearted African Marigold may be happy to know that Gertrude Jekyll found them indispensable in her famous herbaceous borders.

Miss Jekyll noted that the most brightly colored *T. erecta* was perfect for the middle section of her borders. This "hot section" she carefully composed of reds and scarlets and framed with two "cool" border ends of grays and purples. She wrote that "the brilliant orange African Marigold has leaves of a rather dull green, but look steadily at the flowers for thirty seconds in sunshine and then the leaves will appear bright blue."

The moral of this tale is that passing fashion has ruined many a useful flower. Marigold's "naughty smell" is no longer a reason to avoid the flower, and, likewise, its "commonness" should serve as no deterrent to gardeners with good color sense.

Tradescantia virginiana

Tradescantia virginiana was named in honor of John Tradescant the Elder (d. 1637), one of the first great English plant explorers and one of those gardeners never afraid to ask for seeds from this or slips from that. In 1611 he went to work for the first Lord Salisbury in the garden at Hatfield House, and, using this large garden as a base, he began his world-wide search for the best and the most unusual flowers.

English gardens of that period were arranged almost like floral art galleries, and Tradescant's plant treasures so pleased Lord Salisbury that the gardener's likeness was carved into the newel post of Hatfield House's grand staircase. In 1619, the intrepid Tradescant published a book about his plant-travels in Russia, and only one year later, he went to North Africa and returned with the apricot. In 1629, he became Royal Head Gardener to King Charles I and began to search for plants suitable for the English royal gardens. To this end, he "volunteered" his son, John Tradescant the Younger, for the perilous journey to the New World. Being the object of paternal career-boosting must have set well with John the Younger. By 1654, he had made three journeys to Virginia, and in 1656, he published one of the most mouthwatering catalogs of the time, featuring plant after plant of Tradescant introduction.

Spiderwort, photographed at Monticello, was one of the first New World flowers to be taken to England.

John Parkinson, Royal Botanist to Charles I, was very straightforward about how *Tradescantia* got its name: "Upon this plant I confesse that I first imposed the name." He also wrote that it was not actually collected in Virginia by the younger Tradescant, but "received . . . of a friend," but he acknowledged that "the Christian world is indebted to that painful and industrious lover of all Nature's varieties, John Tradescant." Parkinson also wrote that the flower's common name was Spiderwort, but those with arachnophobia should be reassured that whoever decided that the foliage of this plant looked like a tangle of spider's legs must have had the D.T.s. Or perhaps a practitioner of the Doctrine of Signatures realized that there were few cures for spider bite, and, squinting a bit, decided that Tradescantia could fill that prescription if only it could be linked to spiders. The Doctrine of Signatures was uniformly incorrect—and in fact, the sap of Tradescantia can be a very strong skin irritant—but the name Spiderwort unfortunately remains to terrify the timid.

The three-petaled flower of Tradescantia is a lovely blue and nestles close to the grass-like foliage. It winks open in early morning, but starts to retreat into itself if the sun gets very bright. By evening the flower disappears completely, leaving behind the little dab of watery jelly that gives the plant the folk name Widow's Tears.

Tradescantia is invaluable ground cover for poor, shaded, wet soils where it makes a tangled mass of leaves. Although it has been described as "stalwart and effective from a distance, but disappointing at close range," it is quite charming when planted in clumps with Honesty and Jacob's-Ladder (*Lunaria annua* and *Polemonium caeruleum*). In addition, this plant celebrates the great exchange of plant material between England and America.

Commelinaceae

SPIDERWORT

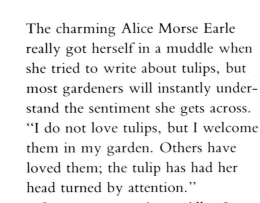

Tulipa batalinii Liliaceae

TULIP

The charming Alice Morse Earle really got herself in a muddle when she tried to write about tulips, but most gardeners will instantly understand the sentiment she gets across. "I do not love tulips, but I welcome them in my garden. Others have loved them; the tulip has had her head turned by attention."

In more recent times, Allen Lacy got right to the gist of the tulip in a *New York Times* article by stating that there are two types of tulip: "the public tulip" and "the private tulip." The public tulip is what Miss Earle despised, those civic displays of tulips that testify as Mr. Lacy says, "with enormous force to the achievements wrought by hybridiz-ers in Holland since the early seventeenth century." Private tulips are those "in the home garden . . . as nature made them, not gussied up by the hand of man."

Two names are associated with the tulip's introduction to the West. Ogier Ghiselin de Busbecq was the Viennese ambassador to the Ottoman court of Suleiman the Great during the middle of the sixteenth century. His job description primarily involved keeping the land-greedy Suleiman from warring, and he did that job admirably. Like most ambassadors in those days, he also found time to conduct a bit of his own business, and was responsible for rescuing the original Codex Ju-

The dainty T. batalinii *is an early-flowering wild tulip that will bloom for many years. Its delicate form, color, and scent charm those visiting Wave Hill in New York in springtime.*

liana of Dioscorides' *De Materia Medica* (along with other priceless classical manuscripts abandoned in Constantinople). He shipped Arab horses home, and introduced lilacs and horse chestnuts to Europe, but his most memorable export was the tulip, which he sent to Emperor Ferdinand I of Germany around 1554. His comments at the time were prophetic: "The Turks cultivate flowers with extreme zeal, and though they are a careful people, do not hesitate to pay a considerable sum for an exceptional flower." He bought a few bulbs "for a great price" and tulip's reputation as a plaything of kings was formed.

Although sources disagree about the dates that de Busbecq began promoting his find to the Emperor, it is safe to say that in a very short time, around 1559, a German naturalist named Konrad von Gesner saw tulips in a garden in Augsburg. Some say the garden belonged to John Harwart, others to Johann Heinrich Howard, others to the family Fugger. In any case, the fact that the tulip was blooming at such an early date in Europe reflected Renaissance enthusiasm for the acquisition of new plants. Whether Harwarts, Howards, or Fuggers, this wealthy family inspired other European landowners to keep up with the Joneses and to acquire the latest tulip varieties from the East for their own gardens.

In 1597, Gerard noted that the tulip had been in England for twenty years and that each year brought so

T. didieri *is another wild tulip whose bulbs are more difficult to obtain than* T. batalinii. *However much you crave these tulips, do not buy bulbs from suppliers who collect from the wild.*

many new colors and varieties from abroad that trying to record them was like "trying to roll Sisyphus's stone or number the sands." The tulip's position in society was documented by Parkinson: "There is no lady or gentlemen of any worth that is not caught with their delight."

Holland, leader in green culture in the 1660s, was the site of the tulip's most infamous reign. From 1634 until 1637, there existed a financial phenomenon never again repeated on such a scale in horticulture—tulipmania. Wilfred Blunt wrote about this disastrous folly in his book *Tulip-*

omania (1950), and explained that, during this period of wild speculation, a nobleman might buy 2,000 florins worth of bulbs from a chimney sweep who had none, and would sell them to a farmer who did not want any, but who planned to sell them to someone else. The whole elaborate gambling scheme was typified by uncontrolled bidding for a red and white tulip called 'Semper Augustus': When everything reached its most frantic pace, there were actually only two bulbs of 'Semper Augustus' in all of Holland. In 1636, tulips were offered on the London Exchange, but good old British reserve prevented much damage from occurring there when the bottom of the market dropped out for Dutch traders the following year. In Holland, many little guys were ruined, a few big guys profited, and, as Buckner Hollingsworth wrote, "the story of Holland's tulipmania had advertised the flower all over Europe better than a modern advertising campaign." Clearly, it was time for tulips to get out of the financial district and back into the garden.

In America, William Byrd, John Custis, and Thomas Jefferson imported, grew, and loved tulips, but from the eighteenth century on, even ordinary gardeners making the average utilitarian effort had tulips. Beginning in the 1830s, this effort by the common man was echoed in northern England, where weavers and factory workers took up growing tulips (and also pinks and auriculas.) The age of the private tulip had dawned at long last.

Choosing old-fashioned tulips for the garden is a matter of sorting through all the options and deciding which flowers suit best. This could take forever. Today there are fifteen divisions of tulips set out in the *Classified List and International Register of Tulip Names.* This tome has an alphabetical listing of all the tulip names that have been published, with specific epithets as well as cultivars. Although it might look a bit daunting to the new gardener, it is no more difficult to use than *Webster's Dictionary.* Among the thousands of tulips documented in the *Classified List* is *Tulipa gesnerana,* originally introduced to England in 1577. It is considered the ancestor of the common Cottage Tulips and was preserved in the cottage gardens so beloved by Margery Fish. The striped and streaked tulips were very popular by 1796 (Maddock's catalog listed 700 varieties) and it is in this group that one would have found the 'King Frederick' Tulip (so beautifully painted by George Ehret) as well as tulipmania's star—'Semper Augustus.' Although the streaked Bizarres, Bybloemens, and Edgers were very popular from an early date, it was not until the 1920s that scientists discovered that a viral disease, and not some sort of alchemy, was responsible for the "breaking" of colors. Because of the big business of tulips, many, many old varieties are still available today, including 'Keizerskroon' (1750), one of the

Some modern tulips such as these from the mid-season-blooming Triumph class are very pretty, but the "civic tulip" has no place in the gently colored spring garden.

earliest named varieties.

There are lots of tulips to wonder about and worry over; for the beginner, there seems to be no one place to start a tulip collection. Consequently, one must firmly rein in all aesthetic anxieties, choose one tulip and buy two dozen bulbs to plant this autumn. Why not start from the beginning and choose a wild tulip? Louise Wilder, in her book *Adventures with Hardy Bulbs* (1936), quoted a very elderly bulb expert as claiming that "if he lived to the age of Methuselah, he might be able to say something definite about the species

and wild forms of tulips, but not until then." The wild tulips have not had their heads turned by too much attention, and their grace and scent charm all those who are weary of the public tulip.

The ancient Turkish ideal tulip had pointed petals colored red or yellow, and *Tulipa batalinii* sweetly fits this description. Native to the Tashkent region, it was named by Edward August von Regal in the mid-nineteenth century. An early, single flower, *batalinii* makes a great choice for the beginning tulip grower.

T. batalinii is small, usually around 4 to 6 inches (10 cm to 15 cm) tall, with a stout, sturdy stem. Four or five leaves grow from each plant and create a blue-green thicket that is just barely topped with perfect little turbans of blooms. The flower is beautifully formed, and is the best sort of yellow—creamy golden with pink tones. *Tulipa batalinii* has a lovely scent, and, planted once, will reappear in the garden year after year.

When all the bulbs have been planted and cold weather means fewer trips to the garden, promise to spend every minute by the fireside, studiously weighing which antique tulips to add next year. And, of course, dream of that chilly spring dawn, when the whole family throws coats and boots over nightwear and has a pre-breakfast walk to see, as Emerson did, "The gardens fire with a joyful blaze/ Of tulips in the morning's rays."

Viola violaceae

Viola cornuta
HORNED PANSY
Viola tricolor
JOHNNY-JUMP-UP
HEARTSEASE

Legend has it that Zeus created violas as food for his lover, Io. He had changed the poor girl into a heifer to conceal their affair from his wife and perhaps it is this deceit that began the tangled web that enmeshes the names connected with this genus.

Strictly speaking, violas, violets, violettas, and pansies are all *Violas.* As one botanical scholar tried to explain, "The difference between a pansy and a viola is a question that puzzles many a garden lover who is not enlightened by the statement that while all pansies are violas, not all violas are suitable for classification as pansies." To simplify matters, the two species considered here will be those that already existed before the frenzy of viola breeding that occurred just after the turn of the nineteenth century: *Viola cornuta* arrived from Switzerland in 1776 and *Viola tricolor* is the ancient Johnny-Jump-Up or Heartsease, native to Europe.

Before 1800, violas were not considered ornamental, but a dishonorably discharged British naval officer, who ostensibly took to gardening for therapy, was soon to change this. Lord Gambier must have done something awfully unmentionable because quite a few books pointedly refuse to be particular about his crime ("discharged with ignominy"; "discharged under somewhat trying circumstances"). But the same texts clearly state that while Lord Gambier turned to flowers for solace, all credit for successful flower breeding on his estate rightfully belonged to his gardener, William Thompson. In 1835, Mr. Thompson crossed the native *Viola tricolor* with another wild viola to create 'Beauty of Ivor,' the first Show Pansy. This blue-faced flower immediately stirred Victorian sentiment and a fad was in full force before one could say viola/violet/etc.

By 1841, there were 400 named

Viola cornuta, OPPOSITE, *makes clusters of foliage and flowers for months. It is a good ground cover and self-seeds successfully.*

varieties of Show Pansy and the Hammersmith Heart's-Ease Society arranged its first show. The English had very strict rules guiding one toward breeding perfect Show Pansies, and it was this rigidity that, perhaps, led the Belgians to develop their own game, the Fancy Pansy. The French were not far behind with Bugloss Blotched, and soon pan-European passion for pansy breeding was uncontrollable. Blooms were so enormous that the flowers could no longer hold their faces out of the soil and pansies became suitable solely for the show table.

At this point, a younger generation of gardeners began clamoring for flowers with better garden effect. Dr. Stuart of Edinburgh commenced crossing Show Pansies with *Viola cornuta* to start a new garden-worthy race. He named them Tufted Pansies, but for some obscure reason, the gardening world simply refused to call Dr. Stuart's creations by the name he preferred, and much to his chagrin and everyone else's confusion, these plants became generally known as violas.

When one feels like giving up on growing violas/etc., for fear of never being able to find the way through such a confusion of names, it is time to take advice from an old, confident Yankee. In 1896, Elias Long wrote *"Viola cornuta* and *Viola tricolor* are hardy plants of highest attractiveness . . . easily grown, very ornamental, and inexpensive,"* and of the thousands of named varieties available during his time, he singled out these two humble ancestors as perfect for "Beautifying Homes, Rural Districts, Towns, and Cemeteries." From Long's sagacious tone, the amateur gardener should gain confidence that these two are worth growing.

Viola cornuta has been called Horned Pansy, Horned Violet, and Mountain Pansy. It seems that this name confusion will rear its ugly head again and again, so perhaps it is best to call this flower *V. cornuta* and nothing else. These sweetly scented, long-spurred flowers—pale blue, mauve, and white—were praised by William Robinson for their wonderful habit of "waving everywhere like thousands of little banners." For the lucky gardener, this alpine native will bloom intermittently from April until frost. It is easy to grow, and if protected by shade will make a good ground cover by producing verdant

Viola tricolor, *Johnny-Jump-Up, at Wave Hill,* LEFT. *Violas have undergone extensive breeding; two well-loved hybrids are Irish Molly,* ABOVE, *and Jackanapes,* BELOW.

mounds of leaves. In some climates it may need to be treated as an annual, but *V. cornuta* will come true from self-sown seed. Margery Fish especially liked growing pale blue *V. cornuta* next to Lady's Mantle *(Alchemilla vulgaris)* and she noted with delight that this charming plant will work its way up through the taller Lady's Mantle to mingle its flowers with its living support.

Viola tricolor is the pansy Shakespeare said was for thoughts (probably from the French *pensée),* but one probably does not want to think about the fact that old Johnny-Jump-Up

has more than 200 common names. It is Heartsease, Herb Trinity, Three-faces-in-a-hood, Love-in-idleness, Pink-of-my-Joan, Kiss-me-at-the-garden-gate, and Tickle-my-fancy. *Viola tricolor* also holds the record for the longest folk name, Meet-Her-In-The-Entry-Kiss-Her-In-The-Buttery, and with this final extravaganza, silence will prevail about violas and names.

Medieval Europeans ate salads of wild onions and violas and one can easily grow enough of this flower to make a stylish splash in party vegetables. Jefferson grew *V. tricolor* at Shadwell in 1767, and a chronicler of his garden wrote that the freely seeding plant appeared "in such unexpected places as to charm the soberest of gardeners."

This dainty plant has combinations of yellow, purple, blue, cream, and white on its small flowers, and the dark, delicate lines on the face, called honey guides, recall Milton's "pansy freak'ed with jet." *Viola tricolor* is actually a short-lived perennial, best grown in rich soil and cool shade. Rotate plants every few years to avoid root disease and otherwise, just deadhead for continuous bloom.

Gerard wrote about *V. tricolor's* one drawback, "the stalkes are weak and tender," but this legginess can be overcome if, once a month, all flowers are picked to give the plant a rest. One can either make a charming little flower arrangement, or, like Io, eat the whole bunch and muse on getting back to basics.

Alchemilla vulgaris

USDA ZONES 3 THROUGH 9

Ambergate Gardens s; Bachman's Nursery s; Garden Place s; Holbrook Farm & Nursery p; Logee's Greenhouses p; Rocknoll Nursery s; Schlichenmayer's Old Farm Nursery, Inc. s; Shady Acres Nursery s; Springbrook Gardens, Inc. s; Thompson & Morgan s; Wayside Gardens s; Well-Sweep Herb Farm p; White Flower Farm p.

Aquilegia vulgaris

USDA ZONES 3 THROUGH 9

Environmental Seed Producers, Inc. s,p; Little Valley Wholesale Nursery s; Seeds Blüm s; Select Seeds, s; TJCHP s; Thompson & Morgan s.

Aruncus dioicus

USDA ZONES 4 THROUGH 8

Kurt Bluemel, Inc. s; Busse Gardens s; Carroll Gardens s; Gardens of the Blue Ridge s; Holbrook Farm & Nursery p; J.L. Hudson s,p; Plantage, Inc. s; Planter's Palette s; Shady Oaks Nursery s; Sunny Border Nurseries, Inc. s; Thompson & Morgan s; Wayside Gardens s; We-Du Nurseries p; White Flower Farm p.

Calendula officinalis

ANNUAL

Environmental Seed Producers, Inc. s,p; Harris' Seeds s; Heirloom Gardens s; J.L. Hudson s; Select Seeds, s; TJCHP s; Thompson & Morgan s; Well-Sweep Herb Farm p.

Campanula medium

BIENNIAL

W. Atlee Burpee, Co. s; Farmer Seed & Nursery s; Harris' Seeds s,p; J.L. Hudson s,p; Northrup King s,p; Geo. W., Park Seed Co., Inc., s; Planter's Palette s; Swedberg Nurseries, Inc. s; Thompson & Morgan s; Well-Sweep Herb Farm p.

Centaurea cyanus

ANNUAL

Abundant Life Seed Foundation s; W. Atlee Burpee, Co. s; Environmental Seed Producers, Inc. s,p; Harris' Seeds s; Native

Where to Find the Flowers

s = SEEDS; p = PLANTS; b = BULBS

Addresses and telephone numbers of sources mentioned below are given in Nurseries section immediately following. See p. 160 for USDA zone map.

Plants, Inc. s,p; Clyde Robin Seed Co., Inc. s,p; Thompson & Morgan s.

Centranthus ruber

USDA ZONES 6 THROUGH 9

Bluebird Nursery, Inc. s; Kurt, Bluemel, Inc. s; Carroll Gardens s; Forestfarm s; Garden Place s; J.L. Hudson, s,p; Little Valley Wholesale Nursery s; Planter's Palette s; Schlichenmayer's Old Farm Nursery, Inc. s; Shady Oaks Nursery s; Sunny Border Nurseries, Inc. s; Thompson & Morgan s; Wayside Gardens s; Well-Sweep Herb Farm p; White Flower Farm p.

Cheiranthus cheiri

USDA ZONES 6 THROUGH 8

Canyon Creek Nursery, p; The Country Garden, s; TJCHP s; Thompson & Morgan s.

Chrysanthemum parthenium

USDA ZONES 6 THROUGH 10

Abundant Life Seed Foundation s; Camelot North Greenhouses & Nursery s; Environmental Seed Producers, Inc. s,p; J.L. Hudson, s,p; Heirloom Gardens s; Logee's Greenhouses p; Montrose Nursery p; Thompson & Morgan s; Well-Sweep Herb Farm p.

Corydalis lutea

USDA ZONES 5 THROUGH 9

Lamb Nurseries, p; Montrose Nursery p; Thompson & Morgan s.

Crambe cordifolia

USDA ZONES 6 THROUGH 9

Canyon Creek Nursery, p; The Fragrant Path, p; J.L. Hudson, s,p; Lamb Nurseries, p; Wayside Gardens p.

Dianthus barbatus

BIENNIAL

Bachman's Nursery s; W. Atlee, Burpee Co. s,p; Carroll Gardens s; J.W. Jung Seed Co. s; Orchid Gardens s; Geo. W. Park Seed Co., Inc. s; Schlichenmayer's Old Farm Nursery, Inc. s; Sunny Border Nurseries, Inc. s; Thompson & Morgan s.

Dianthus deltoides

USDA ZONES 4 THROUGH 8

Aubin Nurseries, Ltd. s; Camelot North Greenhouses & Nursery s; J.L. Hudson, s,p; Native Plants, Inc. s,p; Orchid Gardens s,p; Schlichenmayer's Old Farm Nursery, Inc. s; Stokes Seeds, Inc. s; Sunny Border Nurseries, Inc. s; Thompson & Morgan s; White Flower Farm p.

Dianthus plumarius

USDA ZONES 4 THROUGH 8

Carroll Gardens s; Eisler Nurseries s; Gilson Gardens s; Harris' Seeds s; J.W. Jung Seed Co. s; Little Valley Wholesale Nursery s; Montrose Nursery p; Planter's Palette s; Stokes Seeds, Inc. s; Sunny Border Nurseries, Inc. s; Thompson & Morgan s; Wayside Gardens p.

Dicentra spectabilis

USDA ZONES 3 THROUGH 9

Ambergate Gardens s; Aubin Nurseries, Ltd. s; Bachman's Nursery s; Bailey Nurseries, Inc. s; Bluebird Nursery, Inc. s; Kurt Bluemel, Inc. s; W. Atlee Burpee, Co. s; Camelot North Greenhouses & Nursery s; Busse Gardens s; Carroll Gardens s; Cooper's Garden s; Country Gardens, Inc. s; Cross Nurseries, Inc. s; Farmer Seed & Nursery s; Garden Place s; Gilson Gardens s; Green Value Nursery s; A.M. Grootendorst, Inc. s; Holbrook Farm & Nursery p; Jewell Nurseries, Inc. s; Lake County Nursery Exchange s; Little Valley Wholesale Nursery s; Maple Leaf Gardens s; Native Plants Inc. s; Northland Nursery s; Geo W. Park Seed Co., Inc.

s,p; Plantage, Inc. s; Planter's Palette s; Rocknoll Nursery s; Schlichenmayer's Old Farm Nursery, Inc. s; Swedberg Nurseries, Inc. s; Thompson & Morgan s; Wayside Gardens p; White Flower Farm p.

Digitalis purpurea

USDA ZONES 4 THROUGH 8

Bluebird Nursery, Inc. s; Carroll Gardens s; Eisler Nurseries s; Environmental Seed Producers, Inc. s,p; Holbrook Farm & Nursery p; J.L. Hudson s,p; J.W. Jung Seed Co. s; Native Plants, Inc. s,p; Clyde Robin Seed Co., Inc. s,p; Thompson & Morgan s; Wayside Gardens p; Well-Sweep Herb Farm p; White Flower Farm p.

Dipsacus fullonum

BIENNIAL

Bluebird Nursery, Inc. s; J.L. Hudson s,p; Thompson & Morgan s; Well-Sweep Herb Farm p.

Eremurus robustus

USDA ZONES 6 THROUGH 9

McClure & Zimmerman b.

Fritillaria meleagris

USDA ZONES 4 THROUGH 8

DeJager, Peter, Bulb Co. b; French's b; Hudson, J.L. b,p; Lyon, John D., Inc. b; McClure & Zimmerman b; Thompson & Morgan s; Van Bourgondien Bros. b; Wayside Gardens b; White Flower Farm p.

Gladiolus byzantinus

USDA ZONES 6 THROUGH 10

McClure & Zimmerman b; Van Bourgondien Bros. b.

Hesperis matronalis

USDA ZONES 3 THROUGH 8

Bluebird Nursery, Inc. s; Camelot North Greenhouses & Nursery s; Environmental Seed Producers, Inc. s,p; Harris' Seeds s,p; Heirloom Gardens s; Maple Leaf Gardens s; Native Plants, Inc. s,p; Geo. W. Park Seed Co., Inc. s; Seeds Blüm s; Thompson & Morgan s.

Iberis sempervirens

USDA ZONES 3 THROUGH 9

Aubin Nurseries, Ltd. s; Bluebird Nursery, Inc. s; Kurt Bluemel, Inc. s; W. Atlee Burpee, Co. s,p; Busse Gardens s; Camelot North Greenhouses & Nursery s; Carroll Gardens s; Country Gardens, Inc. s; Eisler Nurseries s; Environmental Seed Producers, Inc. s,p; Garden Place s; Gilson Gardens s; A.M. Grootendorst, Inc. s; Harris' Seeds s,p; Holbrook Farm & Nursery p; J.L. Hudson s,p; Little Valley Wholesale Nursery s; Maple Leaf Gardens s; Native Plants Inc. s; Northrup King s,p; Geo. W. Park Seed Co., Inc. s,p; Springbrook Gardens, Inc. s; Sunny Border Nurseries, Inc. s; Thompson & Morgan s; Wayside Gardens p; White Flower Farm p.

Iberis umbellata

ANNUAL

W. Atlee Burpee, Co. s; Harris Seeds s; Geo. W. Park Seed Co., Inc. s; Stokes Seeds, Inc. s; Thompson & Morgan s.

Lilium lancifolium

USDA ZONES 4 THROUGH 8

W. Atlee Burpee, Co. b; J.W. Jung, Seed Co. b; Thompson & Morgan b; Van Bourgondien Bros. b; Wayside Gardens b.

Lunaria annua

BIENNIAL

Bluebird Nursery, Inc. s; W. Atlee Burpee, Co. s; Harris' Seeds s; Maple Leaf Gardens s; Northrup King s,p; Stokes Seeds, Inc. s; Sunny Border Nurseries, Inc. s; Thompson & Morgan s.

Lysimachia punctata

USDA ZONES 5 THROUGH 8

Bachman's Nursery s; Bluebird Nursery, Inc. s; Forestfarm s; Garden Place s; J.L. Hudson s,p; Maple Leaf Gardens s; Northland Nursery s; Plantage, Inc. s; Planter's Palette s; Shady Oaks Nursery s; Springbrook Gardens, Inc. s; Sunny Border Nurseries, Inc. s; Thompson & Morgan s; White Flower Farm p.

Lythrum salicaria

USDA ZONES 3 THROUGH 9

Abundant Life Seed Foundation s; Environmental Seed Producers, Inc. s,p; J.L. Hudson s,p; Little Valley Wholesale Nursery s; Schlichenmayer's Old Farm Nursery, Inc. s; William Tricker, Inc. s; Wayside Gardens p; White Flower Farm p.

Macleaya cordata

USDA ZONES 4 THROUGH 9

Bluebird Nursery, Inc. s; Kurt Bluemel, Inc. s; Busse Gardens s; Carroll Gardens s; Garden Place s; Plantage, Inc. s; Planter's Palette s; Springbrook Gardens, Inc. s; Sunny Border Nurseries, Inc. s; Well-Sweep Herb Farm p.

Meconopsis cambrica

USDA ZONES 6 THROUGH 9

J.L. Hudson s,p; Thompson & Morgan s.

Narcissus poeticus

USDA ZONES 4 THROUGH 8

McClure & Zimmerman b; Van Bourgondien Bros. b; White Flower Farm p.

Nicotiana alata

USDA ZONES 8 THROUGH 10

Harris' Seeds s; Geo. W. Park Seed Co., Inc. s; Seeds Blüm s; TJCHP s; Thompson & Morgan s.

Papaver nudicaule

USDA ZONES 3 THROUGH 8

W. Atlee Burpee, Co. s,p; Camelot North Greenhouses & Nursery s; Environmental Seed Producers, Inc. s,p; Little Valley Wholesale Nursery s; Maple Leaf Gardens s;

Native Plants, Inc. **s**; Geo. W. Park Seed Co., Inc. **s**; Schlichenmayer's Old Farm Nursery, Inc. **s**; Seeds Blüm **s**; Stokes Seeds, Inc. **s**; Thompson & Morgan **s**.

Papaver orientale
USDA ZONES 3 THROUGH 8
W. Atlee Burpee, Co. **s,p**; Geo. W. Park Seed Co., Inc. **s**; Seeds Blüm **s**; Thompson & Morgan **s**; Well-Sweep Herb Farm **p**; White Flower Farm **p**.

Papaver rhoeas
ANNUAL
Abundant Life Seed Foundation **s**; W. Atlee Burpee, Co. **s**; Environmental Seed Producers, Inc. **s,p**; Heirloom Gardens **s**; J.L. Hudson **s,p**; Native Plants, Inc. **s,p**; Geo. W. Park Seed Co., Inc. **s**; Clyde Robin, Seed Co., Inc. **s,p**; Thompson & Morgan **s**.

Papaver somniferum
ANNUAL
The Country Garden **s**; TJCHP **s**; Thompson & Morgan **s**.

Phlomis samia
USDA ZONES 6 THROUGH 8
Kurt Bluemel, Inc. **s**; Thompson & Morgan **s**.

Polemonium caeruleum
USDA ZONES 4 THROUGH 8
Abundant Life Seed Foundation **s**; Bachman's Nursery **s**; Camelot North Greenhouses & Nursery **s**; Forestfarm **s**; J.L. Hudson **s,p**; Geo. W. Park Seed Co., Inc. **s,p**; Planter's Palette **s**; Rocknoll Nursery **s**; Shady Oaks Nursery **s**; Schlichenmayer's Old Farm Nursery, Inc. **s**; Sunny Border Nurseries, Inc. **s**; Thompson & Morgan **s**; We-Du Nurseries **p**; White Flower Farm **s,p**.

Primula vulgaris
USDA ZONES 5 THROUGH 8
Montrose Nursery **p**; Geo. W. Park Seed Co., Inc. **s**; Thompson & Morgan **s**.

Pulmonaria officinalis
USDA ZONES 3 THROUGH 8
Canyon Creek Nursery **p**; Lamb Nurseries **p**; Well-Sweep Herb Farm **s,p**.

Rosa rugosa
USDA ZONES 2 THROUGH 8
Abundant Life Seed Foundation **s**; Bailey Nurseries, Inc. **s**; Berthold Nursery **s**; Brehm's Wonder Creek Nursery **s**; Carroll Gardens **s**; Concord Nurseries, Inc. **s**; Country Gardens, Inc. **s**; Forestfarm **s**; Forest Nursery Co. **s**; Green Value Nursery **s**; Hanchar's Superior Trees **s**; Hess' Nurseries, Inc. **s**; J.L. Hudson **s,p**; Ingleside Plantation Nurseries **s**; Kankakee Nursery Co. **s**; V. Kraus Nurseries, Ltd. **s**; Lake County Nursery **s**; Lawyer Nursery, Inc. **s**; LBG Nursery **s**; Monrovia Nursery Co. **s**; Plantage, Inc. **s**; Sunny Border Nurseries, Inc. **s**; Thompson & Morgan **s**; Wayside Gardens **p**.

Salvia sclarea
BIENNIAL
Abundant Life Seed Foundation **s**; Carroll Gardens **s**; Heirloom Gardens **s**; J.L. Hudson **s,p**; Logee's Greenhouses **p**; Geo. W. Park Seed Co., Inc. **s,p**; Thompson & Morgan **s**; Wayside Gardens **p**; Well-Sweep Herb Farm **p**.

Saxifraga umbrosa
USDA ZONES 7 THROUGH 9
Select Seeds **s**; Thompson & Morgan **s**.

Sedum telephium
USDA ZONES 4 THROUGH 9
Holbrook Farm & Nursery **p**; Lamb Nurseries, **p**; Wayside Gardens **p**; White Flower Farm **p**.

Stachys byzantina
USDA ZONES 5 THROUGH 9
Bluebird Nursery, Inc. **s**; Kurt Bluemel, Inc. **s**; Northrup King **s,p**; Planter's Palette **s**; Shady Acres Nursery **s**; Thompson & Morgan **s**; Well-Sweep Herb Farm **p**.

Tagetes erecta
ANNUAL
J.L. Hudson **s**; TJCHP **s**.

Tagetes patula
ANNUAL
W. Atlee Burpee, Co. **s**; TJCHP **s**.

Tradescantia virginiana
USDA ZONES 4 THROUGH 9
Gardens of the Blue Ridge **s**; We-Du Nurseries **p**.

Tulipa batalinii
USDA ZONES 5 THROUGH 9
Peter DeJager Bulb Co. **b**; Holbrook Farm & Nursery **b**; McClure & Zimmerman **b**; White Flower Farm **p**.

Viola cornuta
USDA ZONES 5 THROUGH 8
W. Atlee Burpee, Co. **p**; Environmental Seed Producers, Inc. **s,p**; J.W. Jung Seed Co. **s**; Geo. W. Park Seed Co., Inc. **s**; Sunny Border Nurseries, Inc. **s**; Thompson & Morgan **s**; White Flower Farm **p**.

Viola tricolor
USDA ZONES 4 THROUGH 8
Bachman's Nursery **s**; W. Atlee Burpee, Co. **s**; Heirloom Gardens **s**; J.L. Hudson **s,p**; Geo. W. Park Seed Co., Inc. **s,p**; Shady Acres Nursery **s**; Sunny Border Nurseries, Inc. **s**; TJCHP **s**; Thompson & Morgan **s**; Well-Sweep Herb Farm **p**.

Nurseries

All sources are retail except where specified as wholesale.

ABUNDANT LIFE SEED FOUNDATION
P.O. Box 772
Port Townsend, WA 98368
(206) 385-5660

AMBERGATE GARDENS
8015 Krey Ave.
Waconia, MN 55387
(612) 443-2248

AUBIN NURSERIES, LTD.
Box 1089
Carman, Manitoba RoG oJo
Canada
(204) 745-6703

BACHMAN'S NURSERY
6010 Lyndale Ave. So.
Minneapolis, MN 55419
(612) 861-7676

BAILEY NURSERIES, INC.
1325 Bailey Rd.
St. Paul, MN 55119
(612) 459-9744
Wholesale

BERTHOLD NURSERY
434 East Devon Ave.
Elk Grove Village, IL 60007
(312) 439-2600

BLUEBIRD NURSERY, INC.
515 Linden St.
Clarkson, NE 68629
(402) 892-3457
Wholesale

KURT BLUEMEL, INC.
2740 Greene La.
Baldwin, MD 21013
(301) 557-7229

BLUESTONE PERENNIALS, INC.
7211 Middle Ridge Rd.
Madison, OH 44057

BREHM'S WONDER CREEK NURSERY
N6050 So. Crystal Lake Rd.
Beaver Dam, WI 53916
(414) 885-4300
Retail/Wholesale

W. ATLEE BURPEE, CO.
300 Park Ave.
Warminster, PA 18974
(215) 674-4915

CAMELOT NORTH GREENHOUSES &
NURSERY
R.R. 2 Box 398
Pequot Lakes, MN 56472
(218) 568-8922

CANYON CREEK NURSERY
3527 Dry Creek Rd.
Oroville, CA 95965

CARROLL GARDENS
444 East Main St.
P.O. Box 310
Westminster, MD 21157
(301) 848-5422

CONCORD NURSERIES, INC.
Mileblock Rd.
North Collins, NY 14111
(716) 337-2485
Wholesale

COOPER'S GARDEN
212 W. Country Rd.
Roseville, MN 55113
(612) 484-7878

THE COUNTRY GARDEN
Route 2, Box 455A
Crintz, WI 54114

COUNTRY GARDENS, INC.
450 So. Service Rd.
Melville, NY 11747
(516) 694-0131
Wholesale

CROSS NURSERIES, INC.
19774 Kenwood Trail West
Lakeville, MN 55044
(612) 469-2414
Wholesale

PETER DeJAGER BULB CO.
P.O. Box 2010
188 Asbury St.
South Hamilton, MA
(617) 468-4707

EISLER NURSERIES
Route 422
Prospect, PA 16052
(412) 865-2830

ENVIRONMENTAL SEED
PRODUCERS, INC.
P.O. Box 5904
El Monte, CA 91734
(818) 442-3330
Wholesale

FARMER SEED & NURSERY
818 N.W. 4th St.
Faribault, MN 55021
(507) 334-1623
Retail/Wholesale

FORESTFARM
990 Tetherow Rd.
Williams, OR 97544
(503) 846-6963

FOREST NURSERY CO.
Route 2 Box 118-A
McMinnville, TN 37110
(615) 473-2133
Wholesale

THE FRAGRANT PATH
P.O. Box 328
Fort Calhoun, NE 68023

FRENCH'S
Route 100
Pittsfield, VT 05762
(802) 746-8148

GARDEN PLACE
6780 Heisley Rd.
P.O. Box 388
Mentor, OH 44060
(216) 255-3705

GARDENS OF THE BLUE RIDGE
P.O. Box 10
Pineola, NC 28662
(704) 733-2417

GILSON GARDENS
P.O. Box 277
3059 U.S. Route 20
Perry, OH 44081
(216) 259-4845
Wholesale

GREEN VALUE NURSERY
3180 Edgerton St.
Vadnais Heights, MN 55110
(612) 483-1176

GRIFFREY'S NURSERY
1670 Highway 25-70
Marshall, NC 28753
(704) 656-2334

A.M. GROOTENDORST, INC.
P.O. Box 787
Benton Harbor, MI 49022
(616) 925-2535

HANCHAR'S SUPERIOR TREES
P.O. Box 407
Carrolltown, PA 15722
(814) 472-4382
Wholesale

HARRIS' SEEDS
Moreton Farm
3670 Buffalo Rd.
Rochester, NY 14624
(716) 594-9411

HEIRLOOM GARDENS
P.O. Box 138
Guerneville, CA 95446
(707) 869-0967

HESS' NURSERIES, INC.
Route 553
P.O. Box 326
Cedarville, NJ 08311
(609) 447-4213
Wholesale

HOLBROOK FARM & NURSERY
Route 2 Box 223B
Fletcher, NC 28732
(704) 891-7790

J.L. HUDSON
P.O. Box 1058
Redwood City, CA 94064

INGLESIDE PLANTATION NURSERIES
P.O. Box 1038
Oak Grove, Va 22443
(804) 224-7111
Wholesale

JEWELL NURSERIES, INC.
P.O. Box 457
Lake City, MN 55041
(612) 345-3356
Wholesale

J.W. JUNG SEED CO.
335 So. High St.
Randolph, WI 53957-0001
(414) 326-3121

KANKAKEE NURSERY CO.
P.O. Box 288
Aroma Park, IL 60910
(815) 973-9358
Wholesale

V. KRAUS NURSERIES, LTD.
Carlisle
Ontario L0R 1H0
Canada
(416) 689-4022
Wholesale

LAKE COUNTY NURSERY
EXCHANGE
Route 84 Box 122
Perry, OH 44081
(216) 259-5571
Wholesale

LAMB NURSERIES
East 101 Sharp Ave.
Spokane, WA 99202
(509) 328-7956

LAWYER NURSERY, INC.
950 Highway 200 West
Plains, MT 59859
(406) 826-3881
Wholesale

LBG NURSERY
Route 5, Box 130
Princeton, MN 55371
(612) 389-4920

LITTLE VALLEY WHOLESALE
NURSERY
13022 East 136th Ave.
Brighton, CO 80601
(303) 659-6708
Wholesale

LOGEE'S GREENHOUSES
55 North St.
Danielson, CT 06239
(203) 774-8035

LOWE'S OWN-ROOT ROSES
6 Sheffield Rd.
Nashua, NH 03062

JOHN D. LYON, INC.
143 Alewife Brook Parkway
Cambridge, MA 02140
(617) 876-3705

MAPLE LEAF GARDENS
10162 93rd Ave. North
Maple Grove, MN 55369
(612) 428-2640
Wholesale

McCLURE & ZIMMERMAN
1422 West Thorndale
Chicago, IL 60660
(312) 989-0557

MONROVIA NURSERY CO.
18331 East Foothill Blvd.
Azusa, CA 91702
(818) 334-9321
Wholesale

MONTROSE NURSERY
P.O. Box 957
Hillsborough, NC 27278
(919) 732-7787

MULTIFLORA IMPORT CO.
P.O. Box 603
Wayzata, MN 55391
(612) 475-1124
Wholesale

NATIVE PLANTS INC.
417 Wakara Way
Salt Lake City, UT 84108
(800) 533-8498

NICHOLS GARDEN NURSERY
1190 North Pacific Highway
Albany, OR 97321

NORTHLAND NURSERY
16700 Pueblo Blvd.
Jordan, MN 55352
(612) 492-2867

NORTHRUP KING
P.O. Box 959
7500 Olson Memorial Highway
Minneapolis, MN 55440
(612) 593-7394

ORCHID GARDENS
6700 Splithand Rd.
Grand Rapids, MN 55744
(218) 326-6975

GEO. W. PARK SEED CO., INC.
Cokesbury Rd.
P.O. Box 46
Greenwood, SC 29648-0046
(803) 223-7333

PLANTAGE, INC.
P.O. Box 28
Cutchoque, NY 11935
(516) 734-6832
Wholesale

PLANTER'S PALETTE
28 West 521 Roosevelt Rd.
Winfield, IL 60190
(312) 293-1040

OTTO RICHTER AND SONS, LTD.
Goodwood, Ontario
LOC 1AO
Canada

CLYDE ROBIN SEED CO., INC.
P.O. Box 2366
Castro Valley, CA 94545
(415) 581-3467

ROCKNOLL NURSERY
9210 U.S. 50
Hillsboro, OH 45133
(513) 393-1278

JOHN SCHEEPERS, INC.
63 Wall St.
New York, NY 10005

SCHLICHENMAYER'S OLD FARM
NURSERY, INC.
5550 Indiana St.
Golden, CO 80403
(303) 278-0754

SEEDS BLÜM
Idaho City Stage
Boise, ID 83706
(208) 324-0858

SELECT SEEDS
81 Stickney Hill Road
Union, CT 06076

SHADY ACRES NURSERY
7777 Highway 212
Chaska, MN 55318
(612) 466-3391
Retail/Wholesale

SHADY OAKS NURSERY
700-19th Ave. N.E.
Waseca, MN 56093

SPRINGBROOK GARDENS, INC.
6776 Heisley Rd.
P.O. Box 388
Mentor, OH 44061
(216) 255-3059
Wholesale

STOKES SEEDS, INC.
Box 548
Buffalo, NY 14240
(416) 688-4300

SUNNYBROOK FARMS NURSERY
9448 Mayfield Rd.
P.O. Box 6
Chesterland, OH 44026

SUNNY BORDER NURSERIES, INC.
1709 Kensington Rd.
P.O. Box 86
Kensington, CT 06037
(203) 828-0321
Wholesale

SWEDBERG NURSERIES, INC.
P.O. Box 418
Battle Lake, MN 56515
(218) 864-5526

THE THOMAS JEFFERSON CENTER
FOR HISTORIC PLANTS (TJCHP)
Monticello
P.O. Box 316
Charlottesville, VA 22902

THOMPSON & MORGAN
P.O. Box 1308
Jackson, NJ 08527
(201) 363-2225

WILLIAM TRICKER, INC.
7125 Tanglewood Dr.
P.O. Box 31267
Independence, OH 44131
(216) 524-3491

VAN BOURGONDIEN BROS.
P.O. Box A
245 Farmingdale Rd.
Route 109
Babylon, NJ 11702
(800) 645-5830
(800) 832-5689

ANDRE VIETTE FARM AND NURSERY
Rt. 1,
Box 16
Fishersville, VA 22939

VIETTE'S NURSERIES
Rt. 25A
East Norwich, NY 11732

WAYSIDE GARDENS
Hodges, SC 29695-0001
(800) 845-1124

WE-DU NURSERIES
Route 5 Box 724
Marion, NC 28752
(704) 738-8300

WELL-SWEEP HERB FARM
317 Mt. Bethel Rd.
Port Murray, NJ 07865
(201) 852-5390

WHITE FLOWER FARM
Litchfield, CT 06759-0050
(203) 469-9600

Societies and Educational Organizations

ANDERSON HORTICULTURAL
LIBRARY
3675 Arboretum Dr.
Chanhassen, MN 55317

ASSOCIATION FOR LIVING
HISTORICAL FARMS AND
AGRICULTURAL MUSEUMS
Smithsonian Institution
Washington, DC 20560

ASSOCIATION FOR THE
PRESERVATION OF VIRGINIA
ANTIQUITIES (APVA)
2300 East Grace St.
Richmond, VA 23223

BAILEY HORTORIUM
Cornell University
Ithaca, NY 14850

HARDY PLANT SOCIETY
Mid-Atlantic Chapter:
Mrs. Jean Schumacher
49 Green Valley Rd.
Wallingford, PA 19086

INSTITUTE FOR HISTORIC
HORTICULTURE
150 White Plains Rd.
Tarrytown, NY 10591

LONGWOOD LIBRARY
Longwood Gardens
Kennett Square, PA 19348

MASSACHUSETTS HORTICULTURAL
LIBRARY
300 Massachusetts Ave.
Boston, MA 02115

NATIONAL AGRICULTURAL CENTER
Special Collections
10301 Baltimore Blvd.
Beltsville, MD 20705

NATIONAL COLONIAL FARM
Accokeek, MD 20607

NATIONAL TRUST FOR HISTORIC
PRESERVATION
1785 Massachusetts Ave., N.W.
Washington, DC 20036

NATURAL RESOURCES DEFENSE
COUNCIL
1350 New York Ave., N.W.
Washington, DC 20005

PENNSYLVANIA HORTICULTURAL
LIBRARY
325 Walnut St.
Philadelphia, PA 19106

SEED SAVERS EXCHANGE
P.O. Box 70
Decorah, IA 52101

SHIELDS LIBRARY
University of California
Davis, CA 95616

SMITHSONIAN INSTITUTION
Historic Research Division
Washington, DC 20560

SOCIETY FOR THE PRESERVATION OF
NEW ENGLAND ANTIQUITIES
141 Cambridge St.
Boston, MA 02114

SOUTHERN GARDEN HISTORY
ASSOCIATION
Mrs. Zachery T. Bynum
Old Salem, Inc.
Drawer F, Salem Station
Winston-Salem, NC 27101

THE THOMAS JEFFERSON CENTER
FOR HISTORIC PLANTS
Monticello
P.O. Box 316
Charlottesville, VA 22902

Other contacts include but are not
limited to:

Agricultural Extension Agencies
Agricultural Museums
Arboreta
Botanical Gardens
College and University Libraries,
    Herbaria and Departments of
    Horticulture, Agriculture and
    Floriculture
Garden Clubs
Historical Farms and Museums
Historical Societies
Horticultural Societies
Plant Societies

Bibliography

Addison, Josephine. 1985. *The Illustrated Plant Lore*. London: Sidwick & Jackson.

Allen, R.C. 1948. *Roses for Every Garden*. New York: M. Barrows & Co.

Andersen Horticultural Library's Source List of Plants and Seeds. 1987. By Richard T. Isaacson and the Andersen Horticultural Library, n.p., Andersen Horticultural Library.

Anderson, A.W. 1950. *The Coming of the Flowers*. London: Williams & Norgate Ltd.

Anderson, Frank J. 1981. *Cultivated Flowers*. New York: Abbeville Press.

Bailey, Lee. 1985. *Lee Bailey's Country Flowers*. New York: Clarkson N. Potter.

Banks, Roger. 1983. *Old Cottage Garden Flowers*. England: World's Work Ltd: Windmill Press.

Belts, Edwin Morris. 1944. *Thomas Jefferson's Garden Book, 1766–1824*. Philadelphia: American Philosophical Society.

Bentham, George. 1908. *The British Flora*. London: Lovell Reeve, & Co.

Berkeley, Edmund, and Dorothy Smith Berkeley. 1982. *The Life and Travels of John Bartram: From Lake Ontario to the River St. John*. Tallahassee: University Presses of Florida.

Berrall, Julia S. 1966. *The Garden*. New York: The Viking Press.

Betts, Edwin M., and Hazlehurst Bolton Perkins. 1986. *Thomas Jefferson's Flower Garden at Monticello*. Virginia: University of Virginia Press.

Blanchan, Neltje. 1913. *The American Flower Garden*. New York: Doubleday, Page & Co.

———. 1900. *Nature's Garden*. New York: Garden City Publishing Co.

———. 1924. *Wild Flowers Worth Knowing*. New York: Doubleday, Page & Co.

Blanchini, Francesco, and Francesco Corbetta. 1915. *The Complete Book of Health Plants*. New York: Crescent Books.

Blunt, Wilfrid. *Tulipomania*. 1950. Middlesex, England: Penguin Books.

Bourne, Eleanor. n.d. *Heritage of Flowers*. New York: G.P. Putnam's Sons.

Bray, Lys de. 1984. *Lys de Bray's Manual of Old-Fashioned Flowers*. Somerset, England: Oxford Illustrated Press.

———. 1986. *Old-Fashioned Shrubs*. Sparkford, England: Oxford Illustrated Press.

Brett, Walter. 1939. *Your Garden's Flowers Illustrated*. London: C. Arthur Pearson, Ltd.

Brickell, Christopher, and Fay Sharman. 1986. *The Vanishing Garden: A Conservation Guide to Garden Plants*. London: John Murray and the Royal Horticultural Society.

Bowles, E.A. 1914. *My Garden in Summer*. New York: Dodge Publishing.

Bunyard, Edward A. 1937. *Old Garden Roses*. London: Country Life.

Camps, Wendell, et al. 1957. *The World In Your Garden*. Washington, D.C.: National Geographic Society.

Carter, Tom. 1984. *The Victorian Garden*. Salem: Salem House.

Cassels, John. 1987. "The Historic Plant Center at Monticello." In *Early American Life Gardens Book*, n.p., p. 40.

Chelsea Physic Garden. 1986. London: The Chelsea Society.

Childs, Ann, and Stanley Coleman. n.d. *Say It with Flowers and Plants*. New York: Avenel Books.

Christopher, Thomas. "A new chapter on information for perennials." *New York Times*, May 31, 1987, Pastimes Sec., p. 56.

———. "Antique flowers." *House & Garden*, Dec. 1984, p. 74.

———. "On the trail with Texas rose rustlers." *Horticulture*, Aug. 1987, p. 24.

Coats, Alice M. 1956. *Flowers and Their Histories*. New York: Pitman Press.

———. 1968. *Flowers and Their Histories*. London: Adam & Charles Black.

Cook, E.T., ed. n.d. *The Century Book of Gardening: A Comprehensive Work for Every Lover of the Garden*. London: Country Life: George Newness, Reprint 1980, Darby, Pennsylvania: Arden.

Culpeper, Nicholas. 1653 *Culpeper's Complete Herbal*, Reprint 1960, Hackensack, New Jersey: Wehman.

Dobson, Beverly R. 1987. *The Combined Rose List*. Irvington: Dobson.

———. A popularity poll. *Bev Dobson's Rose Letter*, No. 6.

Dodge, Bertha S. 1959. *Plants That Changed the World*. Boston: Little, Brown & Co.

Downing, A.J. 1865. *A Treatise On the Theory and Practice of Landscape Gardening Adapted to North America: With a View to the Improvement of Country Residences*. New York: Orange Judd Co.

Dutton, Joan Parry. 1979. *Plants of Colonial Williamsburg: How to Identify 200 of Colonial America's Flowers, Herbs and Trees*. Virginia: The Colonial Williamsburg Foundation.

Earle, Alice Morse. 1901. *Old Time Gardens*. New York: MacMillan.

Ely, Helena Rutherfurd. 1913. *A Woman's Hardy Garden*. New York: MacMillan.

Faust, Joan Lee. "A new incentive for restoration." *New York Times*, Sept. 27, 1987, Pastimes Sec., p. 69.

Favretti, Rudy J. 1984. *Long Range Master Plan for Bartram's Garden*.

Fish, Margery. 1965. *A Flower for Every Day*. London: Faber & Faber.

———. 1961. *Cottage Garden Flowers*. London: W.H. & L. Collingridge Ltd.

Folsom, James P. "Botany: From myth to method." *Pacific Horticulture*, Fall 1987, p. 44.

Fraser, J., and L. Hemsley. 1846. *Johnson's Gardener's Dictionary and Cultural Instructor*. London: George Rontledge & Sons.

From Seed to Flower: Philadelphia 1681–1876: A Horticultural Point of View. 1976. Philadelphia: Pennsylvania Horticultural Society.

Garden Club of America donates collection to Smithsonian. *Bulletin of American Garden History,* Summer, 1987, p. 1.

Genders, Roy. 1960. *Bulbs All the Year Round.* London: Garden Book Club.

———. [1969] 1984. *The Cottage Garden and the Old-Fashioned Flowers.* London: Pelham Books.

———. n.d. *The Rose: A Complete Handbook.* New York: Bobbs-Merrill Co., Inc.

Gerard, John. 1633. *The Herball or Generall Historie of Plantes,* Gathered by John Gerarde of London, Master in Chirurgerie, very Much Enlarged and Amended by Thomas Johnson Citizen and Apothecarye of London. Reprint 1975, New York: Dover.

Gorer, Richard. 1975. *The Flower Garden in England.* London: B.T. Batsford Ltd.

Graham, Rose, and Peter King, eds. 1986. *Green Words: The Sunday Times Book of Garden Quotations.* London: Quartet Books.

Gray, Asa. 1887. *The Elements of Botany.* New York: Ivison, Blakeman & Co.

Harding, Alice Edward. 1923. *Peonies in the Little Garden.* Boston: Atlantic Monthly Press.

Hatch, Peter. 1987. *Chainyballs, Tennis-balls, and the Breast of Venus: Searching for the Plants of Thomas Jefferson.* n.p.

Hay, Rod, ed. 1985. *Reader's Digest Encyclopedia of Garden Plants & Flowers.* London: The Reader's Digest Association.

Hervey, E.W. 1860. *A Catalogue of Plants Found in New England and Its Vicinity: Arranged According to the Season of Their Flowering.* New Bedford: Press of E. Anthony.

Hobhouse, Penelope. 1985. *Color in Your Garden.* Boston: Little, Brown & Co.

Hollingsworth, Buckner. 1958. *Flower Chronicles.* New Jersey: Rutgers University Press.

———. 1962. *Her Garden Was Her Delight.* New York: MacMillan.

Hortus Third. 1976. By the Staff of the Liberty Hyde Bailey Hortorium. New York: MacMillan Co.

Hunt, William Lanier. "Reflowering Dixie." *Rodale's Organic Gardening,* Nov. 1987, p. 95.

———. A review of *Gardening for Love,* by Elizabeth Lawrence. *Organic Gardening Magazine,* Oct. 1987, p. 28.

Hyams, Edward. 1964. *The English Garden.* London: Thames & Hudson.

Jackson, Bernard S. "Newfoundland's heirloom flower garden." *Garden,* Nov./Dec. 1986, p. 12.

———. "Oxen Pond Botanic Park." *Garden,* Nov./Dec. 1981, p. 6.

Jacobs, Katharine L. "Celia Thaxter and her island garden." *Landscape,* 1980, Vol. 24, No. 3.

Johnson, Hugh. 1979. *The Principles of Gardening.* New York: Simon & Schuster.

Joyce, Edward J. "Thomas Jefferson, gardener." *Rodale's Organic Gardening,* March 1986, p. 42.

Klimas, John E., and James E. Cunningham. 1974. *Wildflowers of Eastern America.* New York: Galahad Books.

Lacy, Allen. 1984. *Home Ground: A Gardener's Miscellany.* New York: Ballantine Books.

———. "Today's interest in gardens of the past." *New York Times Magazine,* Oct. 18, 1987, Part II, p. 12.

Larsen, Marsha. "George Washington's garden." *Early American Life Gardens Book,* 1987, p. 42.

———. "The oldest garden in America." *Early American Life Gardens Book,* 1987, pp. 42–43.

Lawrence, Elizabeth. 1987. *Gardening for Love: The Market Bulletins.* Durham: Duke University Press.

———. 1942. *A Southern Garden: A Handbook for the Middle South.* Chapel Hill: University of North Carolina Press; revised 1984.

Lounsberry, Alice. 1899. *A Guide to the Wild Flowers.* New York: Frederick A. Stokes.

Leighton, Ann. 1986. *American Gardens in the Eighteenth Century: "For Use or for Delight."* Amherst: University of Massachusetts Press.

———. 1987. *American Gardens in the Nineteenth Century: "For Comfort and Affluence."* Amherst: University of Massachusetts Press.

———. 1986. *Early American Gardens: For Meate or Medicine.* Amherst: University of Massachusetts Press.

———. "Re-creating a seventeenth century garden." *House & Garden,* July 1987, p. 20.

Long, Elias A. 1896. *Ornamental Gardening for Americans.* New York: Orange Judd Co.

Lord, Tony, ed. 1987. *The Plant Finder.* Whitbourne, England: Headmain Ltd.

MacSelf, A.J. 1935. *Sanders': The Flower Garden.* London: W.H. & L. Collingridge.

Marshall, Elizabeth D. "Plants of yesteryear." *Pacific Horticulture,* Fall 1987, p. 43.

Massingham, Betty. 1982. *A Century of Gardeners.* London: Faber & Faber.

McClure, Susan A. 1987. "A mid-nineteenth century garden re-created in the western reserve." *Bulletin of American Garden History,* Summer 1987, p. 8.

McCurdy, Robert M. 1917. *Garden Flowers.* New York: Doubleday.

McFarlan, Jan. "Plantings for a 17th century garden in the 20th century." *The Green Scene,* March 1987, p. 24.

McLean, Elizabeth. n.d. *George Washington Takes Tea at Gray's Ferry.* n.p.

McMahon, Bernard. 1806. *The American Gardener's Calendar.* Philadelphia; Reprint ed., Little Compton, RI: Theophrastus.

Mitchell, Henry. "Rare species." *House & Garden,* Oct. 1987, p. 56.

Mower, D.R., Jr. 1987. *Bartram's Garden.* Philadelphia: The John Bartram Association.

Newcomb, Peggy C. 1985. *Popular Annuals of Eastern North America 1865–1914.* Washington, D.C.: Dumbarton Oaks.

Nichols, Beverly. 1963. *Garden Open Today.* New York: E.P. Dutton & Co.

———. 1956. *Sunlight on the Lawn.* London: Johnathan Cape.

Nicholson, George. 1888. *The Illustrated Dictionary of Gardening,* Vols. I, IV, V, and VIII of *An Encyclopedia of Horticulture.* London: L. Upcott Gill.

Page, Russell. 1983. *The Education of A Gardener.* New York: Random House.

Parkinson, John. 1629. *Paradisi in Sole Paradisus Terrestris.* Reprint 1975, New York: Dover.

Parmentier, Andre. n.d. Landscapes & picturesque gardens. From *The New American Gardener,* by Thomas Fessenden. In *Bulletin of American Garden History,* p. 12.

Perry, Frances. 1972. *Flowers of the World.* New York: Hamlyn.

Puryear, Pamela Ashworth. "A Texas cottage garden: Tales of a collector." *Bulletin of American Garden History*, n.d., p. 14.

Ridge, Antonia. n.d. *The Man Who Painted Roses*. London: Faber & Faber

Robinson, William. 1906. *The English Flower Garden and Home Grounds*. London: John Murray.

Rockwell, F.F. 1951. *Gladiolus*. New York: MacMillan Co.

Rothschild, Miriam, and Clive Farrell. 1983. *The Butterfly Gardener*. London: Michael Joseph.

Ryskamp, Charles, and Ruth Hayden and Alice Hufstader. 1986. *Mrs. Delany's Flower Collages from the British Museum*. New York: The Pierpont Morgan Library.

Salisbury, The Most Honourable the Marchioness of. "An Eden Regained." *House & Garden*, June 1985, p. 124.

Sanecki, Kay N. 1985. *Fragrant and Aromatic Plants*. London: The Royal Horticultural Society.

Sawyer, A. 1986. *The Plant Buyer's Directory*. Salem: Salem House.

Scott-James, Anne. 1981. *The Cottage Garden*. London: Allen Lane, Penguin Books.

Shelton, Louise. 1916. *Beautiful Gardens in America*. New York: Charles Scribner's Sons.

Sitwell, Sacheverell. 1939. *Old Fashioned Flowers*. London: Country Life Ltd.

Snipes, Christy. "The southern Bartram connection." *Bulletin of American Garden History*, Vol. II, No. 2, 1987, p. 19.

Spingarn, Joel E. 1987. A Duchess County gardener's diary: 1829–1866. From Henry Winthrop Sargent and Early History of Horticulture in Duchess County, New York. from *1937 Year Book of Duchess County Historical Society*. In *Bulletin of American Garden Historical Society*, Summer 1987, p. 11.

Steer, William. n.d. *Gardening Encyclopedia*. London: Spring Books

Stuart, David, and James Sutherland. 1987. *Plants from the Past*. New York: Viking.

Swain, Roger B. "What's in a name." *Horticulture*, July 1987, p. 16.

"The Tale A Garden Told." *Early American Life Gardens Book*, 1987, p. 41.

Taylor, Charles. "Apple grower helps save Thomas Jefferson orchard." Roanoke Rapids, North Carolina, *Daily & Sunday Herald*, Oct. 7, 1987, Farm Sec.

Taylor, Raymond L. 1952. *Plants of Colonial Days*. Williamsburg: Colonial Williamsburg Press.

Thaxter, Celia. 1894. *An Island Garden*. Reprint 1985, Ithaca: Bullbrier Press.

Thomas, Graham Stuart. 1956. *Old Shrub Roses*. Boston: Chas. T. Branford Co.

———. 1982. *Perennial Garden Plants: The Modern Florilegium*. London: J.M. Dent & Sons Ltd.

Thomas, H.H. 1912. *The Complete Gardener*. London: Cassell & Co.

Thompson, Al. 1987. "La Parissima Mission colonial revival gardens: Preserve mission era plants." In *Bulletin of American Garden History*, Vol. II, No. 1, p. 11.

Tice, Patricia M. 1984. *Gardening in America 1830–1910*. Rochester: The Strong Museum.

Tozer, Eliot. Review of *Gardening for Love*, by Elizabeth Lawrence. In *Horticulture*, July 1987, p. 66.

Van Ravenswaay, Charles. 1977. *A Nineteenth Century Garden*. New York: Universe Books.

Venison, Tony. "Living a dream: Gardens of Hatfield House." *Country Life*, March 15, 1984, p. 662.

———. "Replanting the past: The gardens of Hatfield House." *Country Life*, March 22, 1984, p. 770.

Von Baeyer, Edwinna. 1984. *Rhetoric and Roses: A History of Canadian Gardening*. Ontario: Fitzhenry & Whiteside.

Weinreb, Herman. "New use for a time-tested botanical." *Garden*, Nov./Dec. 1986, p. 16.

Welebit, Diane. "Among plants, terrors vanish." *Garden*, March/April 1987, p. 28.

White, Christie. Review of *Flores Poetice: The Florist's Manual*, by H. Bourne. *Bulletin of American Garden History*, Summer 1987, p. 10.

Whitsey, Fred. "The Garden We Saved." *Country Life*, Oct. 8, 1987, p. 100.

Whittle, Tyler, and Christopher Cook. 1981. *Curtis's Flower Garden Displayed: 120 Plates from Years 1787–1807*. Oxford: Oxford University Press.

Wright, Richardson. 1924. *The Practical Book of Outdoor Flowers*. New York: Garden City Publishing Co.

———. 1935. *The Story of Gardening From the Hanging Gardens of Babylon to the Hanging Gardens of New York*. New York: Dodd, Mead & Co.

———. 1934. *The Winter Diversions of A Gardener*. Philadelphia: J.B. Lippincott Co.

Index

Numbers in italics indicate illustrations.

‎❧

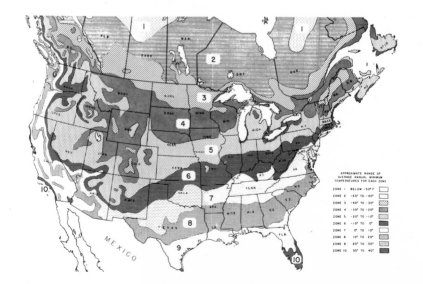